Rankin Surname

Ireland: 1600s to 1900s

From Ireland Church Records of Baptism, Marriage and Death

Comprised of Roman Catholic and Church of Ireland Records

From Counties Carlow, Cork, Kerry and Dublin City

Compiled by **Donovan Hurst**

March 23, 2013

Dedication

This work is dedicated to all of those that came before us and shaped our lives to make us the people that we are today.

Table of Contents

Introduction i

Parish Churches iii

    Carlow (Church of Ireland) iii

    Cork & Ross (Roman Catholic or RC) iii

    Dublin (Church of Ireland) iii

    Dublin (Roman Catholic or RC) iv

    Kerry (Church of Ireland) iv

    Kerry (Roman Catholic or RC) iv

Families 1

Individual Baptisms/Births 52

Individual Burials 53

Individual Marriages 59

Name Variations 68

Notes 70

Index 76

Introduction

This is a compilation of individuals who have the surname of Rankin that lived in the country of Ireland from the 1600s to the 1900s. I have placed each entry into one of four categories: Families, Individual Births/Baptisms, Individual Burials, and Individual Marriages. If a marriage entry primarily concerns an Individual Rankin whom is female, then I have placed that entry under the category of Individual Marriages. If a marriage entry primarily concerns an Individual Rankin whom is male, then I have placed that entry under the category of Families. Images of many of these listings are available at http://churchrecords.irishgenealogy.ie/churchrecords/.

To help guide the reader of this work, the format of this book is as follows:

- Main Family Entry (Husband and Wife) (Father and Mother)

    o Child of Main Family Entry, including Spouse(s) when available

        ▪ Grandchild of Main Family Entry, including Spouse(s) when available

            • Great-Grandchild of Main Family Entry, including Spouse(s) when available

(**Bolded Text**) following any entry includes any additional information such as Residence(s), Occupation(s), Signature(s), etc. when available.

Hurst

Some of the fonts used in this work symbolizes Celtic writing. The traditional letters, numbers, and punctuation marks and their Celtic counterparts are as follows:

Traditional Letters (Uppercase & Lowercase)

A a B b C c D d E f G g H h I i J j K k L l M m N n O o P p Q q R r S s T t U u V v W w X x Y y Z z

Celtic Letters (Uppercase & Lowercase)

A a B b C c D ð E e F ſ G g H h I í J j K k L l M m

N n O o P p Q q R ʀ S s T t U u V ʋ W ω X x Y y Z z

Traditional Numbers

1 2 3 4 5 6 7 8 9 10

Celtic Numbers

1 2 3 4 5 6 7 8 9 10

Traditional Punctuation

. , : ' " & - ( )

Celtic Punctuation

. , : ' " & - ( )

Rankin Surname Ireland: 1600s to 1900s

Parish Churches
Carlow (Church of Ireland)

Carlow Parish and Dunleckney Parish.

Cork & Ross
(Roman Catholic or RC)

Cork - SS. Peter & Paul Parish.

Dublin (Church of Ireland)

Arbour Hill Barracks Parish, Clontarf Parish, Crumlin Parish, Glasnevin Parish, Grangegorman Parish, Kilmainham Parish, North Strand Parish, Richmond Barracks Parish, Rotunda Chapel Parish, St. Andrew Parish, St. Anne Parish, St. Audoen Parish, St. Bride Parish, St. Catherine Parish, St. George Parish, St. James Parish, St. John Parish, St. Mark Parish, St. Mary Parish, St. Nicholas Without Parish, St. Paul Parish, St. Peter Parish, St. Thomas Parish, St. Victor Parish, and Taney Parish.

Dublin (Roman Catholic or RC)

Harrington Street Parish, Rathmines Parish, SS. Michael & John Parish, St. Agatha Parish, St. Andrew Parish, St. Audoen Parish, St. Catherine Parish, St. James Parish, St. Lawrence Parish, St. Mary Parish, St. Mary, Pro Cathedral Parish, St. Michan Parish, and St. Nicholas Parish.

Kerry (Church of Ireland)

Tralee Parish.

Kerry (Roman Catholic or RC)

Spa Parish.

Families

- Alexander Rankin & Mary A. Rankin

  - Alexander Rankin – bapt. 10 Dec 1834 (Baptism, **St. Mary, Pro Cathedral Parish** (RC))

- Charles Rankin & Charlotte Kathrens – 22 Jan 1826 (Marriage, **St. Mary Parish**)

Signatures:

Charles Rankin (husband):

    Residence - St. Mary Parish - January 22, 1826

Charlotte Kathrens (wife):

    Residence - St. Andrew Parish - January 22, 1826

Wedding Witnesses:

Christopher Sharp & William Rankin

Signatures:

- Charles Rankin & Martha Unknown

  - James Rankin – bapt. 9 Apr 1738 (Baptism, **St. Catherine Parish**)

Hurst

- Charles Rankin & Unknown

  o Charles Rankin & Jane Ponsonby Wilson, b. 1837 – 30 Aug 1856 (Marriage, **St. Anne Parish**)

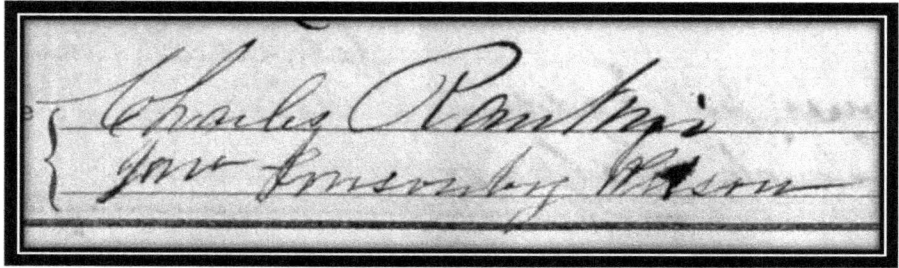

Signatures:

- ▪ Catherine Macgregor Rankin – b. 9 Sep 1874, bapt. 9 Oct 1874 (Baptism, **St. Anne Parish**)

- ▪ Nora Amelia Minnie Rankin – b. 30 Sep 1876, bapt. 2 Nov 1876 (Baptism, **St. Anne Parish**)

- ▪ Allen Ponsonby Rankin – b. 23 Apr 1879, bapt. 10 Jun 1879 (Baptism, **St. Anne Parish**)

- ▪ Spencer Wilson Rankin – b. 15 Jun 1881, bapt. 22 Jul 1881 (Baptism, **St. Anne Parish**)

- ▪ Harold Douglas Rankin – b. 5 Feb 1884, bapt. 28 Mar 1884 (Baptism, **St. Anne Parish**)

Charles Rankin (son):

Residence - 10 Nassau Street - August 30, 1856

12 Nassau Street - October 9, 1874

November 2, 1876

June 10, 1879

13 Nassau Street - July 22, 1881

March 28, 1884

Occupation - Jeweler - August 30, 1856

October 9, 1874

Rankin Surname Ireland: 1600s to 1900s

November 2, 1876

June 10, 1879

July 22, 1881

March 28, 1884

Jane Ponsonby Wilson, daughter of Thomas Wilson (daughter-in-law):

Residence - 11 Nassau Street - August 30, 1856

Age at Marriage - 19 years

Thomas Wilson (father):

Occupation - Manufacturer

Charles Rankin (father):

Occupation - Wine Merchant

Wedding Witnesses:

Joseph S. Wilson & David Armstrong

Signatures:

Hurst

- Charles Edward Rankin & Mary Unknown

  - Mary Rankin – b. 8 Jul 1895, bapt. 14 Jul 1895 (Baptism, **Tralee Parish**)

Charles Edward Rankin (father):

Residence - Tralee - July 14, 1895

Occupation - Sergeant, R. M. Fusiliers - July 14, 1895

- David Rankin & Anne Rankin

  - Jessie Violet Rankin, b. 4 Jun 1862, bapt. 25 Jun 1862 (Baptism, **Grangegorman Parish**) &

    Alexander Lindesay Richardson – 29 Sep 1884 (Marriage, **St. George Parish**)

Signatures:

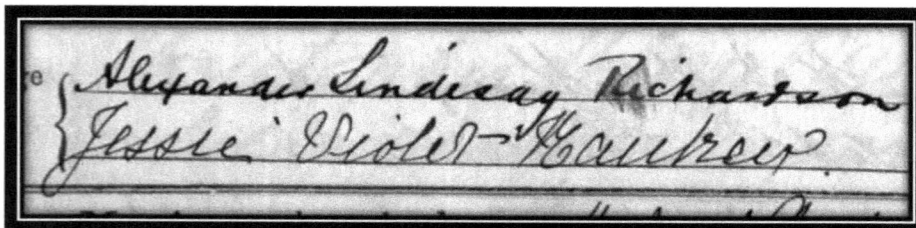

Jessie Violet Rankin (daughter):

Residence - 12 Royal Canal - September 29, 1884

Alexander Lindesay Richardson, son of Effingham L. Richardson (son-in-law):

Residence - 30 Glengariffe Parade - September 29, 1884

Occupation - Compositor - September 29, 1884

Effingham L. Richardson (father):

Occupation - House & Land Agent

Rankin Surname Ireland: 1600s to 1900s

David Rankin (father):

Occupation - Upholsterer

Wedding Witnesses:

Edmund Rankin & Charles Robert Henderson

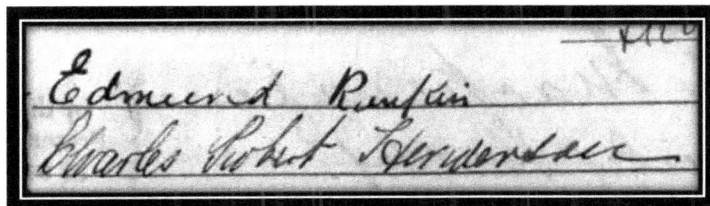

Signatures:

- o David William Rankin – b. 6 Jun 1866, bapt. 12 Aug 1866 (Baptism, **Grangegorman Parish**)

- o Elizabeth Jane Rankin – b. 9 May 1868, bapt. 30 May 1868 (Baptism, **Grangegorman Parish**)

- o William Henry Rankin – b. 14 Nov 1869, bapt. 29 Jan 1870 (Baptism, **Grangegorman Parish**)

- o Henry Rankin – b. 1 Nov 1871, bapt. 7 Feb 1872 (Baptism, **St. George Parish**), bur. 10 Sep 1873 (Burial, **St. George Parish**)

Henry Rankin (son):

Residence - **2 Victoria Terrace, Royal Canal - before September 10, 1873**

Age at Death - **1 year & 10 months**

- o Elizabeth Louisa Rankin – b. 25 Nov 1873, bapt. 14 Jan 1874 (Baptism, **St. George Parish**)

- o Emily Beatrice Rankin – b. 15 Jun 1877, bapt. 5 Sep 1877 (Baptism, **St. George Parish**)

David Rankin (father):

Residence - **3 Catherine Villa on Canal - June 25, 1862**

3 Catherine Villa - August 12, 1866

Hurst

January 29, 1870

February 7, 1872

3 Catherine Villa, Royal Canal - May 30, 1868

2 Victoria Terrace, Royal Canal Bank - January 14, 1874

2 Victoria Terrace - September 5, 1877

Occupation - Upholsterer - June 25, 1862

August 12, 1866

May 30, 1868

January 29, 1870

February 7, 1872

January 14, 1874

September 5, 1877

- David Rankin & Elizabeth Rankin

  o Elizabeth Rankin – b. 28 Jun 1886, bapt. 27 Mar 1889 (Baptism, **St. Thomas Parish**)

  o Sarah Jane Rankin – b. 11 Oct 1889, bapt. 27 Mar 1889 (Baptism, **St. Thomas Parish**)

David Rankin (father):

Residence - 25 Upper Buckingham Street - March 27, 1889

Occupation - Mechanic - March 27, 1889

Rankin Surname Ireland: 1600s to 1900s

- David Rankin & Unknown

  o Elizabeth Rankin & Michael Henry Walshe – 12 Apr 1878 (Marriage, **St. George Parish**)

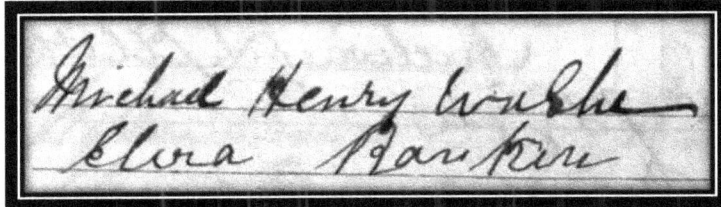

Signatures:

Elizabeth Rankin (daughter):

  Residence - Belmont Place, Middle Gardiner Street - April 12, 1878

Michael Henry Walshe, son of Patrick Walshe (son-in-law):

  Residence - 13 Villa Bank, Royal Bank - April 12, 1878

  Occupation - Stone Mason - April 12, 1878

Patrick Walshe (father):

  Occupation - Carpenter

David Rankin (father):

  Occupation - Stone Mason

Hurst

Wedding Witnesses:

Arthur Bowen & Margery Wheatley

Signatures:

- Edward Rankin & Unknown
  - Mary Rankin & Michael Patrick Browne – 10 Jan 1846 (Marriage, **St. Mary Parish**)

Signatures:

Mary Rankin (daughter):

Residence - 12 Dorset Street - January 10, 1846

Michael Patrick Browne, son of Michael Patrick Browne (son-in-law):

Residence - 12 Dorset Street - January 10, 1846

Occupation - Esquire - January 10, 1846

Relationship Status at Marriage - widow

Michael Patrick Browne (father):

Occupation - Major

Edward Rankin (father):

Occupation - Lieutenant

Wedding Witnesses:

Thomas Courtenay & Mary Courtenay

Signatures:

- Edward Rankin & Unknown
  - Julia Anne Rankin & Bartholomew Martin – 26 Oct 1875 (Marriage, **St. Bride Parish**)

Signatures:

Julia Anne Rankin (daughter):

Residence - Peter Street - October 26, 1875

Bartholomew Martin, son of Richard Martin (son-in-law):

Residence - Peter Street - October 26, 1875

Occupation - Trustworthy Man- October 26, 1875

Hurst

Richard Martin (father):

Occupation - Farmer

Edward Rankin (father):

Occupation - Tradesman

Wedding Witnesses:

Francis Eagan, Michael Walsh, & Margaret Bannington

Signatures:

- Francis Rankin & Arabella Hearn (H e a r n) – 8 Sep 1843 (Marriage, St. George Parish)

Signatures:

   o   Jane Emily Rankin – b. 4 Mar 1845, bapt. 12 Mar 1845 (Baptism, Clontarf Parish)

Francis Rankin (father):

Residence - Annesbrook, Clontarf Parish, Co. Dublin - September 8, 1843

Clontarf - March 12, 1845

Rankin Surname Ireland: 1600s to 1900s

Occupation - Gentleman - September 8, 1843

Esquire - March 12, 1845

Arabella Hearn (mother):

Residence - 15 Portland Street, St. George Parish - September 8, 1843

Wedding Witnesses:

George Hearn & Edward Nugent

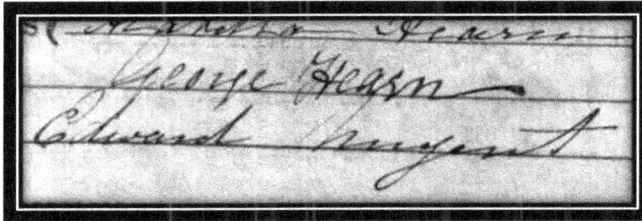

Signatures:

- George Rankin & Anne Jessop
  - Mary Rankin – bapt. 28 Mar 1824 (Baptism, St. Catherine Parish (RC))

- George Rankin & Elizabeth Rankin
  - Anne Georgina Rankin – b. 26 Apr 1870, bapt. 8 May 1870 (Baptism, Rotunda Chapel Parish) (Baptism, St. Mary Parish)

George Rankin (father):

Residence - 8 South Frederick Street - May 8, 1870

Occupation - Clerk in South Dublin Union - May 8, 1870

- George Rankin & Hannah Unknown
  - Christian Rankin – bapt. 25 Jan 1761 (Baptism, St. John Parish)

Hurst

- George Rankin & Harriet Elizabeth Rankin

  - Charlotte Anne Rankin – b. 24 Jan 1861, bapt. 24 Apr 1861 (Baptism, **St. Peter Parish**)

  - George Samuel Rankin – b. 20 Sep 1863, bapt. 11 Nov 1863 (Baptism, **St. Peter Parish**)

  - William Henry Rankin – b. 22 Aug 1865, bapt. 2 Nov 1866 (Baptism, **St. Peter Parish**)

George Rankin (father):

Residence - 16 Heytesbury Street - April 24, 1861

November 11, 1863

November 2, 1866

Occupation - Jeweler - April 24, 1861

November 11, 1863

November 2, 1866

- George Rankin & Isabel Mooney

  - Margaret Rankin – bapt. 19 Jan 1806 (Baptism, **St. James Parish (RC)**)

- George Rankin & Julie Unknown

  - Mary Rankin & Michael Corcoran – 14 Oct 1870 (Marriage, **St. Catherine Parish (RC)**)

Mary Rankin (daughter):

Residence - Temboe - October 14, 1870

Michael Corcoran, son of Michael Corcoran & Margaret Unknown (son-in-law):

Residence - Esker Lodge - October 14, 1870

Wedding Witnesses:

Bernard Dunne & Margaret Reilly

12

Rankin Surname Ireland: 1600s to 1900s

- George Rankin & Julianne Rankin

  - Sarah Rankin & Christopher Burges – 26 Aug 1866 (Marriage, **St. Mary, Pro Cathedral Parish (RC)**)

    - Sarah Burges – b. 9 Feb 1874, bapt. 15 Feb 1874 (Baptism, **St. James Parish (RC)**)

    - John Joseph Burges – b. 14 Apr 1876, bapt. 16 Apr 1876 (Baptism, **St. James Parish (RC)**)

    - Catherine Burges – b. 12 May 1878, bapt. 21 May 1878 (Baptism, **St. James Parish (RC)**)

Sarah Rankin (daughter):

Residence - 202 Britain Street - August 26, 1866

Christopher Burges, son of John Burges & Sarah Burges (son-in-law):

Residence - Thomas Street - August 26, 1866

122 James Street - February 15, 1874

April 16, 1876

May 21, 1878

Wedding Witnesses:

Edward O'Gare & Mary Anne O'Hagan

- George Rankin & Mary Dunn – 22 May 1753 (Marriage, **St. Catherine Parish**)

- George Rankin & Sarah Deegan

  - John Rankin – bapt. 11 Jul 1834 (Baptism, **St. Nicholas Parish (RC)**)

  - Margaret Rankin – bapt. 30 Jun 1835 (Baptism, **St. Catherine Parish (RC)**)

  - Mary A. Rankin – bapt. 20 Aug 1838 (Baptism, **St. Nicholas Parish (RC)**)

Hurst

- George Rankin & Sarah Rankin

  o Margaret Rankin & Gulielmo Ward – 9 May 1858 (Marriage, **St. Mary, Pro Cathedral Parish (RC)**)

    ▪ Mary Teresa Ward – b. 22 Mar 1859, bapt. 8 Apr 1859 (Baptism, **St. Mary, Pro Cathedral Parish (RC)**)

    ▪ Sarah Catherine Ward – b. 17 Jan 1862, bapt. 24 Jan 1862 (Baptism, **St. Mary, Pro Cathedral Parish (RC)**)

Margaret Rankin (daughter):

Residence - 49 Jervis Street - May 9, 1858

Gulielmo Ward, son of Thomas Ward & Anne Ward (son-in-law):

Residence - 65 Barrack Street - May 9, 1858

56 Mary Street - April 8, 1859

6 Jervis Street - January 24, 1862

Wedding Witnesses:

Michael Kavanagh & Mary Mulvey

  o Mary Rankin & John Hughes – 11 Feb 1866 (Marriage, **St. Mary, Pro Cathedral Parish (RC)**)

    ▪ Edward Christopher Hughes, b. 28 May 1866, bapt. 4 Jun 1866 (Baptism, **St. Mary, Pro Cathedral Parish (RC)**) & Julianne Ennis – 8 Feb 1888 (Marriage, **St. Mary, Pro Cathedral Parish (RC)**)

Edward Hughes (son):

Residence - 27 Foster Terrace - February 8, 1888

Rankin Surname Ireland: 1600s to 1900s

Julianne Ennis, daughter of Christopher Ennis & Anne Connor (daughter-in-law):

   Residence - 2 Marlboro Place - February 8, 1888

Wedding Witnesses:

Thomas Cullen & Catherine Walsh

- George Lawrence Hughes – b. 13 Nov 1867, bapt. 18 Nov 1867 (Baptism, **SS. Michael & John Parish** (RC))

- James Hughes – b. 21 May 1869, bapt. 31 May 1869 (Baptism, **St. Michan Parish** (RC))

- Sarah Hughes – b. 16 Feb 1873, bapt. 24 Feb 1873 (Baptism, **St. Mary, Pro Cathedral Parish** (RC))

- John Dominick Hughes – b. 15 Jun 1875, bapt. 21 Jun 1875 (Baptism, **St. Mary, Pro Cathedral Parish** (RC))

- John Hughes – b. 13 Jul 1877, bapt. 23 Jul 1877 (Baptism, **St. Michan Parish** (RC))

- Joseph G. Hughes & Mary Jane Ennis – 20 Jan 1901 (Marriage, **St. Mary, Pro Cathedral Parish** (RC))

Joseph G. Hughes (son):

   Residence - 72 St. Joseph Place - January 20, 1901

Mary Jane Ennis, daughter of John Ennis & Victoria Denham (daughter-in-law):

   Residence - 34 Upper Gloucester Street - January 20, 1901

Wedding Witnesses:

John Ennis & Margaret McKenna

Hurst

Mary Rankin (daughter):

    Residence - 23 Great Strand Street - February 11, 1866

John Hughes, son of Edward Hughes & Elizabeth Hughes (son-in-law):

    Residence - 3 Exchange Court - February 11, 1866

        23 Strand Street - June 4, 1866

        4 Exchange Street - November 18, 1867

        18 Little Britain Street - May 31, 1869

        18 Bolton Street - February 24, 1873

        17 Upper Dorset Street - June 21, 1875

        105 Upper Dorset Street - July 23, 1877

Wedding Witnesses:

Gulielmo O'Brien & Catherine Cullen

- George Rankin & Susan Cleary
  - Francis Rankin – b. 3 Sep 1895, bapt. 9 Sep 1895 (Baptism, St. Mary, Pro Cathedral Parish (RC))

George Rankin (father):

    Residence - 21 Upper Tyrone Street - September 9, 1895

Rankin Surname Ireland: 1600s to 1900s

- George Rankin & Unknown

  ○ Richard Rankin & Anne Martin – 22 Jan 1860 (Marriage, **St. Andrew Parish (RC)**)

    ▪ Mary Emily Rankin – b. 1860, bapt. 1860 (Baptism, **St. Andrew Parish (RC)**)

    ▪ Francis Rankin – b. 1863, bapt. 1864 (Baptism, **St. Andrew Parish (RC)**)

    ▪ Patrick R. Rankin – b. 1866, bapt. 1866 (Baptism, **St. Andrew Parish (RC)**)

    ▪ Anne Rankin – b. 1868, bapt. 1869 (Baptism, **St. Andrew Parish (RC)**)

    ▪ Bridget Rankin – b. 6 Feb 1872, bapt. 9 Feb 1872 (Baptism, **St. Audoen Parish (RC)**)

Richard Rankin (son):

Residence - 60 Lower Mount Street - January 22, 1860

7 Brunswick Place - 1860

1864

1866

1869

17 Ussher Island - February 9, 1872

Anne Martin, daughter of Henry Martin (daughter-in-law):

Residence - 7 Brunswick Place - January 22, 1860

Wedding Witnesses:

John Connor & Margaret McDermott

Hurst

- George Rankin & Unknown

  o Charlotte Anne Rankin & Thomas James Sands – 27 Sep 1883 (Marriage, **Kilmainham Parish**)

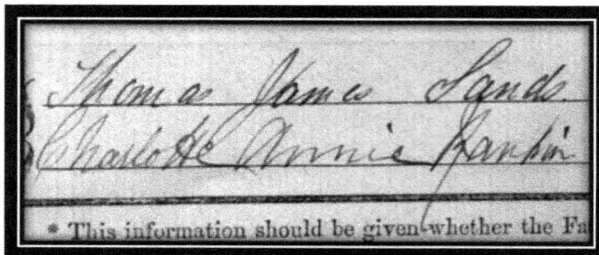

Signatures:

Charlotte Anne Rankin (daughter):

    Residence - Grand Canal - September 27, 1883

Thomas James Sands, son of Joseph Sands (son-in-law):

    Residence - Island Bridge Barracks - September 27, 1883

    Occupation - Corporal, 1st Royal Dragoons - September 27, 1883

Joseph Sands (father):

    Occupation - Commercial Traveller

George Rankin (father):

    Occupation - Clerk

Rankin Surname Ireland: 1600s to 1900s

Wedding Witnesses:

Richard Carr & Elizabeth Carr

Signatures:

- George Rankin & Unknown

  o William Henry Rankin & Helena Parker Catto Cunningham – 1 Feb 1891 (Marriage, **St. Audoen Parish**)

Signatures:

  ▪ Walter George Henry Rankin – b. 26 May 1891, bapt. 30 Jun 1891 (Baptism, **St. Audoen Parish**)

William Henry Rankin (son):

Residence - 5 George's Lane, North Kings Street - February 1, 1891

156 Thomas Street - June 30, 1891

Occupation - Tram Servant - February 1, 1891

Hurst

Stable Man - June 30, 1891

Helena Parker Catto Cunningham, daughter of Andrew Cunningham (daughter-in-law):

Residence - 13 Usher's Island - February 1, 1891

Andrew Cunningham (father):

Occupation - Black Smith

George Rankin (father):

Occupation - Clerk

Wedding Witnesses:

Andrew Cunningham & Thomas Edward Thorpe

Signatures:

- Gulielmo Rankin & Elizabeth Stone
  - Dionysius Rankin & Bridget Clarke – 1 Jul 1873 (Marriage, St. Lawrence Parish (RC))
    - Mary Jane Rankin – b. 15 Sep 1875, bapt. 18 Sep 1875 (Baptism, St. Lawrence Parish (RC))

Dionysius Rankin (son):

Residence - 3 Common Street - July 1, 1873

September 18, 1875

Rankin Surname Ireland: 1600s to 1900s

Bridget Clarke, daughter of Patrick Clarke & Roseanne Carroll (daughter-in-law):

    Residence - 3 Common Street - July 1, 1873

Wedding Witnesses:

John Moore & Anne Murray

- Hamilton Rankin & Catherine Anne Parr – 8 Jul 1820 (Marriage, **St. Paul Parish**)

- Hamilton Rankin & Unknown

  o Emily Anne Rankin & George Read Mac Mullen – 9 Oct 1845 (Marriage, **St. Peter Parish**)

Signatures:

Emily Anne Rankin (daughter):

    Residence - Milltown Colonades - October 9, 1845

George Read Mac Mullen, son of Robert Mac Mullen (son-in-law):

    Residence - Knock Mount, Taney Parish, Dundrun - October 9, 1845

    Occupation - Doctor of Medicine - October 8, 1845

Robert Mac Mullen (father):

    Occupation - Merchant

Hurst

Hamilton Rankin (father):

Occupation - Gentleman

Wedding Witnesses:

John J. Crawford & George Rankin

Signatures:

- Henry Rankin & Elizabeth Rankin

  o Andrew Rankin – b. 27 Jul 1893, bapt. 10 Sep 1893 (Baptism, **St. Paul Parish**)

Henry Rankin (father):

Residence - 47 Montpelier Hill - September 10, 1893

Occupation - Groom - September 10, 1893

- Henry Rankin & Elizabeth Shaw

  o Richard Joseph Rankin – b. 16 Aug 1880, bapt. 23 Aug 1880 (Baptism, **St. Lawrence Parish (RC)**)

Henry Rankin (father):

Residence - 14 Great Foundland Street - August 23, 1880

- Henry Rankin & Helen Rankin

  o Elizabeth Maude Rankin – b. 13 Sep 1896, bapt. 9 Oct 1896 (Baptism, **St. Paul Parish**)

Rankin Surname Ireland: 1600s to 1900s

Henry Rankin (father):

    Residence - 48 South Paul Street - October 9, 1896

    Occupation - Driver D N T Co. - October 9, 1896

- Henry Rankin & Mary Martin – 13 Jan 1857 (Marriage, **St. Andrew Parish (RC)**)
  - Anne Rankin, b. 4 Dec 1859, bapt. 15 Dec 1859 (Baptism, **St. Lawrence Parish (RC)**) & William Sillery – 19 Oct 1879 (Marriage, **St. Mary, Pro Cathedral Parish (RC)**)
    - William Francis Sillery – b. 5 Jan 1885, bapt. 7 Jan 1885 (Baptism, **St. Mary, Pro Cathedral Parish (RC)**)
    - George Sillery – b. 1886, bapt. 1886 (Baptism, **St. Andrew Parish (RC)**)

Anne Rankin (daughter):

    Residence - 27 Mabbot Street - October 19, 1879

William Sillery, son of Henry Sillery & Julie Sheerin (son-in-law):

    Residence - 27 Mabbot Street - October 19, 1879

        47 Lower Mecklenburgh Street - January 7, 1885

        35 Gloucester Street - 1886

Wedding Witnesses:

Henry Rankin & Mary Rankin

  - Mary Rankin – b. 16 Nov 1861, bapt. 25 Nov 1861 (Baptism, **St. Mary, Pro Cathedral Parish (RC)**)
  - Francis Rankin – b. 24 Feb 1864, bapt. 30 Mar 1864 (Baptism, **St. Lawrence Parish (RC)**)

Hurst

- o Bridget Rankin – b. 21 Sep 1866, bapt. 24 Sep 1866 (Baptism, **St. Mary, Pro Cathedral Parish (RC)**)

- o Elizabeth Rankin – b. 15 Feb 1869, bapt. 17 Feb 1869 (Baptism, **St. Lawrence Parish (RC)**)

- o George Rankin – b. 29 Jul 1870, bapt. 1 Aug 1870 (Baptism, **St. Lawrence Parish (RC)**)

- o Richard Rankin – b. 27 Aug 1872, bapt. 27 Aug 1872 (Baptism, **St. Lawrence Parish (RC)**)

- o Patrick Rankin – b. 12 Mar 1874, bapt. 16 Mar 1874 (Baptism, **St. Lawrence Parish (RC)**)

- o John Rankin – b. 11 Apr 1876, bapt. 19 Apr 1876 (Baptism, **St. Lawrence Parish (RC)**)

- o Michael Rankin – b. 11 Feb 1879, bapt. 17 Feb 1879 (Baptism, **St. Mary, Pro Cathedral Parish (RC)**)

- o Henry Rankin & Margaret Browne – 2 Mar 1897 (Marriage, **St. Mary, Pro Cathedral Parish (RC)**)

Henry Rankin (son):

Residence - 33 Lower Mecklenburgh Street - November 25, 1861

22 Mecklenburgh Street - September 24, 1866

18 Montgomery Street - February 17, 1879

15 Upper Tyrone Street - March 2, 1897

Margaret Browne, daughter of Michael Dowd Browne & Ellen Monahan

(daughter-in-law):

Residence - 15 Upper Tyrone Street - March 2, 1897

Wedding Witnesses:

Joseph Kinahan & Mary Lambert

Rankin Surname Ireland: 1600s to 1900s

Henry Rankin (father):

    Residence - 44 Mayor Street - December 16, 1859

        4 Brady's Cottages, Mayor Street - March 30, 1864

        2 Orr's Cottages, Mayor Street - February 17, 1869

        37 Mayor Street - August 1, 1870

        8 Upper Jane Place - August 27, 1872

        2 Lower Jane Place, Oriel Street - March 16, 1874

        3 Emerald Place - April 19, 1876

Wedding Witnesses:

Michael Gormley & Anne Martin

- Hugh Rankin & Elizabeth Unknown
  - James Rankin – b. 4 Nov 1894, bapt. 5 Dec 1894 (Baptism, **St. Catherine Parish**)

Hugh Rankin (father):

    Residence - 7A Ebenezer Terrace - December 5, 1894

    Occupation - Saw Maker - December 5, 1894

- James Rankin & Catherine Brannick
  - Elizabeth Rankin, b. 24 Jan 1877, bapt. 29 Jan 1877 (Baptism, **St. Mary, Pro Cathedral Parish (RC)**) & Arthur Magee – 13 Feb 1901 (Marriage, **St. Mary, Pro Cathedral Parish (RC)**)

Elizabeth Rankin (daughter):

    Residence - 106 Summer Hill - February 13, 1901

Hurst

Arthur Magee, son of John Magee & Margaret Mauchan (son-in-law):

Residence - 72 Lower Gloucester Street - February 13, 1901

Wedding Witnesses:

John Spring & Bridget Maher

- o Catherine Anne Rankin – b. 25 Jul 1879, bapt. 30 Jul 1879 (Baptism, **St. Mary, Pro Cathedral Parish (RC)**)
- o Harriet Rankin – b. 22 Oct 1881, bapt. 26 Oct 1881 (Baptism, **St. Mary, Pro Cathedral Parish (RC)**)

James Rankin (father):

Residence - 10 Upper Gloucester Place - January 29, 1877

10 Lower Gloucester Place - July 30, 1879

October 26, 1881

- James Rankin & Catherine Renwick
  - o Joseph Patrick Rankin – b. 5 Jul 1873, bapt. 9 Jul 1873 (Baptism, **St. Mary, Pro Cathedral Parish (RC)**)

James Rankin (father):

Residence - 17 Gloucester Place - July 9, 1873

- James Rankin & Catherine Rankin
  - o Thomas Rankin – bapt. 21 May 1834 (Baptism, **St. Mary, Pro Cathedral Parish (RC)**)
- James Rankin & Christian Unknown
  - o Margaret Rankin – bapt. 17 Dec 1738 (Baptism, **St. Nicholas Without Parish**)

Rankin Surname Ireland: 1600s to 1900s

James Rankin (father):

Residence - Francis Street - December 17, 1738

- James Rankin & Christian Unknown

    o   Christian Rankin – bapt. 1 Apr 1751 (Baptism, **St. Nicholas Without Parish**)

    o   Jane Rankin –bapt. 20 May 1755 (Baptism, **St. Nicholas Without Parish**)

    o   Esther Rankin – bapt. 27 May 1756 (Baptism, **St. Catherine Parish**)

    o   Susan Rankin – bapt. 6 Nov 1757 (Baptism, **St. Catherine Parish**)

    o   James Rankin – bapt. 1 Mar 1759 (Baptism, **St. Nicholas Without Parish**)

    o   John Rankin – bapt. 21 Jun 1760 (Baptism, **St. Nicholas Without Parish**)

    o   William Rankin – bapt. 13 Sep 1761 (Baptism, **St. Nicholas Without Parish**)

James Rankin (father):

Residence - Francis Street - April 1, 1751

May 20, 1755

March 1, 1759

June 21, 1760

September 13, 1761

- James Rankin & Ellen Collins

    o   William Rankin – bapt. 31 Jan 1834 (Baptism, **St. James Parish (RC)**)

- James Rankin & Jane Curran – 1 Dec 1786 (Marriage, **St. Michan Parish (RC)**)

Wedding Witnesses:

Maurice Lamb & Hannah Curran

Hurst

- James Rankin & Mary Unknown

  o James Rankin – b. 6 Jul 1843, bapt. 5 Mar 1844 (Baptism, **Taney Parish**)

James Rankin (father):

Residence - Villa - March 5, 1844

- James Rankin & Unknown

  o Euphemia Rankin & John Sinclair – 20 Feb 1855 (Marriage, **St. Andrew Parish**)

Signature:

Signatures (Marriage):

- Sarah Mary Sinclair, b. 4 Oct 1895 [Date probably recorded incorrectly], bapt. 7 Sep 1895 (Baptism,

  St. Mary, Pro Cathedral Parish (RC)) & Thomas Byrne (B y r n e) – 8 Sep 1895 (Marriage,

  St. Mary, Pro Cathedral Parish (RC))

Sarah Mary Sinclair (daughter):

Residence - 44 Lower Dominick Street - September 8, 1895

Age at Baptism - adult

Rankin Surname Ireland: 1600s to 1900s

Thomas Byrne, son of Luke Byrne & Bridget King (son-in-law):

    Residence - 51 York Street - September 8, 1895

Wedding Witnesses:

Michael Canan & Jane Sinclair

John Sinclair (father):

    Residence - 44 Lower Dominick Street - September 7, 1895

Euphemia Rankin (daughter):

    Residence - 22 Essex Street - February 20, 1855

John Sinclair, son of Robert Sinclair (son-in-law):

    Residence - 22 Essex Street - February 20, 1855

    Occupation - Printer - February 20, 1855

Robert Sinclair (father):

    Occupation - Land Steward

James Rankin (father):

    Occupation - Lithographic Printer

Hurst

Wedding Witnesses:

John Malone & Thomas O'Connor

Signatures:

o   John Turnbull (T u r n b u l l) Rankin & Helen Clark – 12 Jan 1857 (Marriage, **St. Andrew Parish**)

Signatures:

▪ James Rankin – b. 12 May 1849, bapt. 24 Aug 1862 (Baptism, **St. Mary Parish**)

John Turnbull Rankin (son):

Residence - 22 Essex Street - January 12, 1857

61 Jervis Street - August 24, 1862

Occupation - Lithographer - January 12, 1857

Lithographic Printer - August 24, 1862

Rankin Surname Ireland: 1600s to 1900s

Helen Clark, daughter of James Clark (daughter-in-law):

Residence - 22 Essex Street - January 12, 1857

James Clark (father):

Occupation - Servant

James Rankin (father):

Occupation - Lithographer

Wedding Witnesses:

John Sinclair & Thomas O'Connor

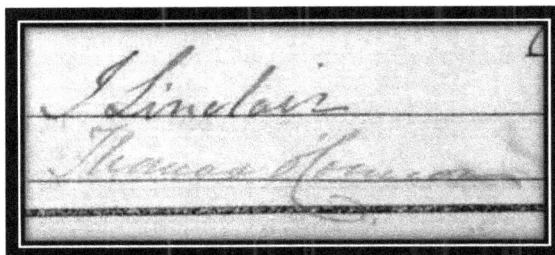

Signatures:

- John Rankin & Agnes Rankin

    o John Rankin – b. 27 Sep 1889, bapt. 6 Oct 1889 (Baptism, **North Strand Parish**)

John Rankin (father):

Residence - 7 King's Avenue - October 6, 1889

Occupation - Bookbinder - October 6, 1889

- John Rankin & Catherine Unknown

    o William Rankin – bapt. 19 May 1817 (Baptism, **St. Mary, Pro Cathedral Parish (RC)**)

Hurst

John Rankin (father):

Residence - 6 Great Britain Street - May 19, 1817

- John Rankin & Eleanor Clarke
  - John Rankin – b. 16 Nov 1852, bapt. 20 Nov 1870 (Baptism, **St. Audoen Parish** (RC))

John Rankin (father):

Residence - 44 Middle Abbey Street - November 20, 1870

- John Rankin & Elizabeth Unknown
  - Mary Rankin – bapt. 1830 (Baptism, **St. Andrew Parish** (RC))
- John Rankin & Elizabeth Unknown
  - Elizabeth Rankin, bapt. 1838 (Baptism, **St. Andrew Parish** (RC)) & Joseph Byrne (B y r n e) – 25 Nov 1856 (Marriage, **St. Nicholas Parish** (RC))
    - Mary Josephine Byrne – b. 8 Dec 1857, bapt. 18 Dec 1857 (Baptism, **St. Nicholas Parish** (RC))

Elizabeth Rankin (daughter):

Residence - 27 Cuffe Street - November 25, 1856

Joseph Byrne, son of Peter Byrne & Elizabeth Unknown (son-in-law):

Residence - 55 Clarendon Street - November 25, 1856

55 Bishop Street - December 18, 1857

Wedding Witnesses:

Peter Whelan & Margaret White

Rankin Surname Ireland: 1600s to 1900s

- John Rankin & Ellen Unknown

  - John Rankin & Roseanne Field – 25 Nov 1877 (Marriage, **St. Michan Parish (RC)**)

    - Elizabeth Rankin – b. 7 Oct 1878, bapt. 9 Oct 1878 (Baptism, **St. Michan Parish (RC)**)

John Rankin (son):

Residence - Ballymahon Street, Longford - November 25, 1877

7 Linen Hall Street - October 9, 1878

Roseanne Field, daughter of Bartholomew Field & Elizabeth Unknown (daughter-in-law):

Residence - 7 Linen Hall Street - November 25, 1877

Wedding Witnesses:

Henry Field & Teresa Field

- John Rankin & Rose McCormick (M c C c r m i c k)

  - John Rankin – b. 22 Jan 1879, bapt. 27 Jan 1879 (Baptism, **SS. Michael & John Parish (RC)**)

John Rankin (father):

Residence - 5 Crampton Quay - January 27, 1879

- John Rankin & Sarah Unknown

  - Elizabeth Rankin – bapt. 1835 (Baptism, **St. Andrew Parish (RC)**)

- John Rankin & Unknown

  - Sydney Rankin & Elizabeth Wheatley – 27 Aug 1867 (Marriage, **St. Mark Parish**)

Signature:

Hurst

Signatures (Marriage):

Sydney Rankin (son):

    Residence - 23 South Cumberland Street - August 27, 1867

    Occupation - Servant - August 27, 1867

Elizabeth Wheatley, daughter of William Wheatley (daughter-in-law):

    Residence - 23 South Cumberland Street - August 27, 1867

William Wheatley (father):

    Occupation - Steward

John Rankin (father):

    Occupation - Land Steward

Wedding Witnesses:

Andrew Webb & Edward Fox

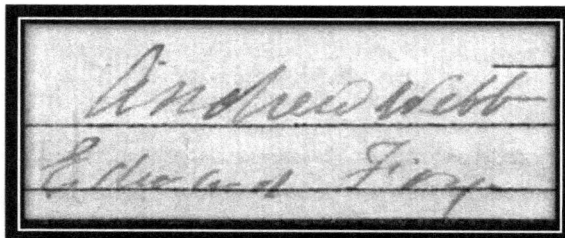

Signatures:

Rankin Surname Ireland: 1600s to 1900s

- Joseph Rankin & Elizabeth Bradford – 2 Sep 1768 (Marriage, **St. Anne Parish**)

- Joseph Rankin & Elizabeth Nicholson

  o Vincent James Rankin – b. 19 Jul 1899, bapt. 31 Jul 1899 (Baptism, **St. Mary, Pro Cathedral Parish (RC)**)

Joseph Rankin (father):

Residence - 9 Capel Street - July 31, 1899

- Joseph Rankin & Unknown

  o Sarah Rankin & James Roy – 5 Nov 1862 (Marriage, **St. Mark Parish**)

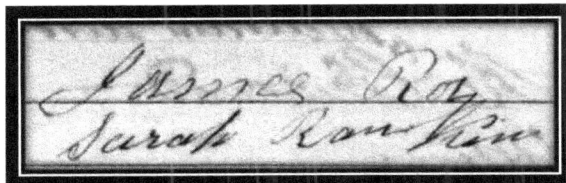

Signatures:

Sarah Rankin (daughter):

Residence - 2 Hamilton Down - November 5, 1862

James Roy, son of Andrew Roy (son-in-law):

Residence - Durrow Parish, Queen's County - November 5, 1862

Occupation - Gentleman - November 5, 1862

Relationship Status at Marriage - widow

Andrew Roy (father):

Occupation - Farmer

Joseph Rankin (father):

Occupation - Farmer

Wedding Witnesses:

James Wingate & Priscilla Straeman

Signatures:

- Leslie Rankin & Unknown
  - James Rankin & Rebecca S. Minion – 9 Dec 1899 (Marriage, **St. Paul Parish**)

Signatures:

James Rankin (son):

Residence - Ligoniel, Belfast - December 9, 1899

Occupation - Constable, R I C - December 9, 1899

Rebecca S. Minion, daughter of Nathaniel Minion (daughter-in-law):

Residence - 23 Arran Quay - December 9, 1899

Nathaniel Minion (father):

Occupation - Farmer

Rankin Surname Ireland: 1600s to 1900s

Leslie Rankin (father):

Occupation - Architect

Wedding Witnesses:

Jeannie Jeffares & Thomas Minion

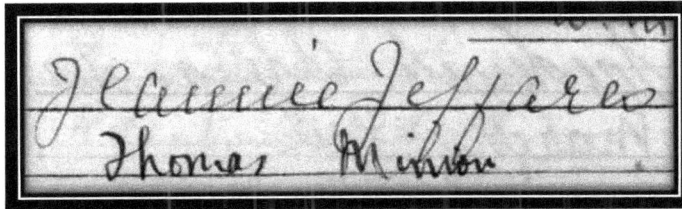

Signatures:

- Nathaniel Rankin & Mary Jane Rankin

    o   William Rankin – bapt. 9 Jan 1859 (Baptism, **Arbour Hill Barracks Parish**)

    o   Elizabeth Constance Rankin – b. 2 Sep 1860, bapt. 30 Sep 1860 (Baptism, **Richmond Barracks Parish**)

Nathaniel Rankin (father):

Residence - Royal Barracks - January 9, 1859

Richmond Barracks - September 30, 1860

Occupation - Sergeant, 76th Regiment - January 9, 1859

Sergeant, 76th Foot - September 30, 1860

- Peter Rankin & Anne Gray – 26 Dec 1835 (Marriage, **St. Andrew Parish (RC)**)

Wedding Witnesses:

Matthew Jones & Julie Reynart

Hurst

- Richard Rankin & Anne Martin
  - George Joseph Rankin & Elizabeth Flanagan – 25 Jun 1893 (Marriage, **Harrington Street Parish (RC)**)
    - Richard Patrick Rankin – b. 20 Oct 1897, bapt. 22 Oct 1897 (Baptism, **St. Mary, Pro Cathedral Parish (RC)**)
    - George Joseph Rankin – b. 6 Feb 1899, bapt. 13 Feb 1899 (Baptism, **St. Mary, Pro Cathedral Parish (RC)**)

George Joseph Rankin (son):

Residence - 3 McMahon Street, South Circular Road - June 25, 1893

    5 Lower Gloucester Street - October 22, 1897

    89 Marlboro Street - February 13, 1899

Elizabeth Flanagan, daughter of Nicholas Flanagan & Mary Magrath (daughter-in-law):

Residence - 51 Daniel Street, Lower Clanbrassil Street - June 25, 1893

Wedding Witnesses:

Richard Rankin & Hannah Cullen

  - Richard Rankin & Margaret Ward – 5 Aug 1895 (Marriage, **Harrington Street Parish** (RC))

Richard Rankin (son):

Residence - 3 McMahon Street - August 5, 1895

Margaret Ward, daughter of Patrick Ward & Roseanne Daly (daughter-in-law):

Residence - 22 Upper Clanbrassil Street - August 5, 1895

Rankin Surname Ireland: 1600s to 1900s

Wedding Witnesses:

Peter Murphy & Mary Read

- Robert Rankin & Anne Unknown
  - Thomas Rankin – bapt. 4 Sep 1837 (Baptism, **St. Mary, Pro Cathedral Parish (RC)**)
- Robert Rankin & Anne Isabel Walsh – 14 Dec 1840 (Marriage, **St. George Parish**)

Signatures:

Robert Rankin (husband):

    Residence - Allaskin Lodge, Co. Donegal - December 14, 1840

    Occupation - Esquire - December 14, 1840

Anne Isabel Walsh (wife):

    Residence - St. George Parish - December 14, 1840

Wedding Witnesses:

John E. Walsh, Henry Bayly, & William T. Rankin

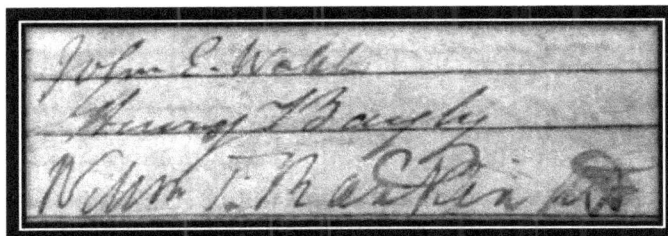

Signatures:

Hurst

- Robert Rankin & Mary Rankin

  o Elizabeth Rankin – bapt. 15 Dec 1766 (Baptism, **St. Mark Parish**)

Robert Rankin (father):

Residence - Moss Street - December 15, 1766

- Robert Rankin & Sarah Rankin

  o James Rankin – bapt. 12 May 1765 (Baptism, **St. Mark Parish**)

Robert Rankin (father):

Residence - Moss Street - May 12, 1765

- Robert Rankin & Sarah Unknown

  o Elizabeth Rankin – b. 1789, bapt. 1789 (Baptism, **St. Andrew Parish (RC)**)

- Samuel James Rankin, d. bef. 13 May 1895 & Unknown

  o Georgina Rankin & Thomas Edmond Hughes – May 13, 1895 (Marriage, **St. Mary Parish**)

Signatures:

Georgina Rankin (daughter):

Residence - 3 Lower Grangegorman - May 13, 1895

Rankin Surname Ireland: 1600s to 1900s

Thomas Edmond Hughes, son of James Hughes (son-in-law):

Residence - 54 Bolton Street - May 13, 1895

Occupation - Gardener - May 13, 1895

Wedding Witnesses:

Frances O'Brien & Thomas Murphy

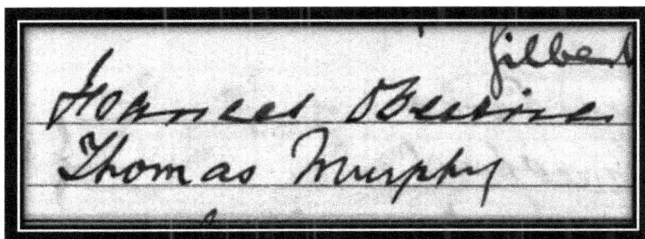

Signatures:

- Thomas Rankin & Jane Rankin

  - Jane Rankin – b. 1807, bapt. 7 Dec 1807 (Baptism, **Carlow Parish**)

  - Abigail Rankin – b. 1810, bapt. 11 Mar 1810 (Baptism, **Carlow Parish**)

- Thomas Rankin & Mary Branagan

  - Catherine Rankin – b. 6 Sep 1874, bapt. 9 Sep 1874 (Baptism, **St. Mary, Pro Cathedral Parish (RC)**)

Thomas Rankin (father):

Residence - Gloucester Diamond - September 9, 1874

- Unknown Rankin & Catherine Rankin

  - Patrick Rankin – b. 1872, bapt. 1872 (Baptism, **St. Andrew Parish (RC)**)

Hurst

Catherine Rankin (mother):

Residence - Lock Hospital - 1872

- Unknown Rankin & Unknown
  - Eva Isabel Rankin – bapt. 2 Apr 1885 (Baptism, **Grangegorman Parish**)

Unknown Rankin (father):

Residence - 39 Prussia Street - April 2, 1885

- Unknown Rankin & Unknown
  - George Rankin

Signature:

- Unknown Rankin & Unknown
  - George Rankin

Signature:

- Unknown Rankin & Unknown
  - James Rankin

Signature:

- Unknown Rankin & Unknown

  o R. B. Rankin

Signature:

- Unknown Rankin & Unknown

  o Susan Rankin

Signature:

- Unknown Rankin & Unknown

  o T. George Rankin

Signature:

- Unknown Rankin & Unknown

  o W. H. Rankin

Signature:

Hurst

- William Rankin & Alice Reynolds – 2 Jul 1713 (Marriage, **St. Andrew Parish**)

- William Rankin & Anne Strait

  o Ellen Rankin – bapt. 2 Jul 1820 (Baptism, **St. Catherine Parish (RC)**)

  o Mary Rankin – b. 3 Aug 1823, bapt. 10 Aug 1823 (Baptism, **St. Catherine Parish (RC)**)

- William Rankin & Anne Strade – 18 Feb 1806 (Marriage, **St. Catherine Parish (RC)**)

  o Teresa Rankin – b. 13 Oct 1809, bapt. 22 Oct 1809 (Baptism, **St. Catherine Parish (RC)**)

Wedding Witnesses:

Michael Goff & Anne Strange

- William Rankin & Janet Rankin

  o Margaret Rankin – b. 27 Dec 1840, bapt. 27 Dec 1840 (Baptism, **St. Mary Parish**)

William Rankin (father):

Residence - **60 Capel Street** - December **27, 1840**

Occupation - **Upholsterer** - December **27, 1840**

- William Rankin & Mary Unknown

  o John David Rankin – b. 8 Dec 1900, bapt. 9 Dec 1900 (Baptism, **St. James Parish**)

William Rankin (father):

Residence - **4 Mount Brown** - December **9, 1900**

Occupation - Compositor - December **9, 1900**

Rankin Surname Ireland: 1600s to 1900s

- William Rankin & Rebecca Rankin

  o Frances Rebecca Rankin – b. 2 Mar 1883, bapt. 16 Mar 1883 (Baptism, **St. Mary Parish**)

  o Mary Rebecca Rankin – b. 14 May 1887, bapt. 18 May 1887 (Baptism, **St. Mary Parish**)

William Rankin (father):

Residence - 1 Upper Abbey Street - March 16, 1883

32 Stafford Street - May 18, 1887

Occupation - Porter - March 16, 1883

May 18, 1887

- William Rankin & Susan Rankin

  o Mary Rankin – bapt. 10 Oct 1740 (Baptism, **St. Mark Parish**)

William Rankin (father):

Residence - George's Street - October 10, 1740

- William Rankin & Unknown

  o Violet Elizabeth Rankin & Thomas Rawson Jenkinson – 5 Apr 1869 (Marriage, **St. George Parish**)

Signatures:

Hurst

Violet Elizabeth Rankin (daughter):

    Residence - 3 Portland Row - April 5, 1869

Thomas Rawson Jenkinson, son of John Jenkinson (son-in-law):

    Residence - 3 Portland Row - April 5, 1869

    Occupation - Upholsterer - April 5, 1869

John Jenkinson (father):

    Occupation - Plumber

William Rankin (father):

    Occupation - Upholsterer

Wedding Witnesses:

William Rankin & Michael Hanlon

Signatures:

Rankin Surname Ireland: 1600s to 1900s

- William Rankin & Unknown

  - Thomas Andrew Rankin & Harriet Lynch – 16 Dec 1883 (Marriage, **St. Mark Parish**)

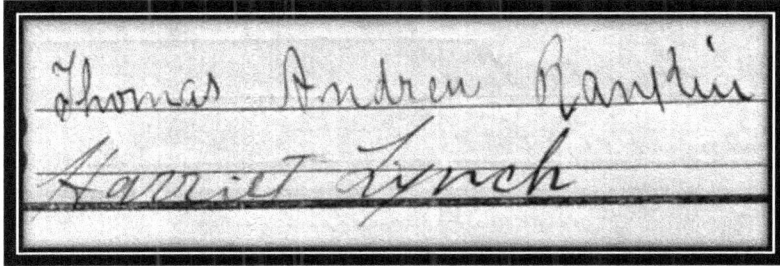

Signatures:

Thomas Andrew Rankin (son):

   Residence - The Ship "Princess Alexandra" - December 16, 1883

   Occupation - Ship Steward - December 16, 1883

Harriet Lynch, daughter of Michael Lynch (daughter-in-law):

   Residence - Kingstown Harbour - December 16, 1883

Michael Lynch (father):

   Occupation - Brick Layer

William Rankin (father):

   Occupation - Head Constable R I C

Wedding Witnesses:

Patrick Lynch & Elizabeth Kirwan

Signatures:

○ Elizabeth Jane Rankin & George Reid – 17 Feb 1885 (Marriage, **St. Peter Parish**)

Signatures:

Elizabeth Jane Rankin (daughter):

Residence - 15 Ely Place - February 17, 1885

George Reid, son of John Reid (son-in-law):

Residence - 42 Heytesbury Street - February 17, 1885

Occupation - Bank Porter - February 17, 1885

Relationship Status at Marriage - widow

John Reid (father):

Occupation - Farmer

Rankin Surname Ireland: 1600s to 1900s

William Rankin (father):

  Occupation - R I Constablary

Wedding Witnesses:

John MacDonald & Edward Kenny

Signatures:

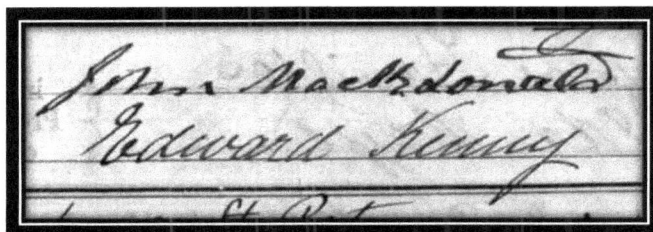

- William Henry Rankin & Violet May Rankin

  o Violet May Rankin – b. 15 Nov 1900, bapt. 23 Dec 1900 (Baptism, **St. Victor Parish**)

William Henry Rankin (father):

  Residence - **24 Hamilton Street** - December **23, 1900**

  Occupation - Telegraphist - December **23, 1900**

- William Humphrey Rankin & Mary Louisa Maunsell – 22 Feb 1845 (Marriage, **St. Peter Parish**)

William Humphrey Rankin (husband):

  Residence - Milltown Colonade - February **22, 1845**

  Occupation - Gentleman - February **22, 1845**

Mary Louisa Maunsell (wife):

  Residence - **7 Ontario Terrace** - February **22, 1845**

  Occupation - Spinster - February **22, 1845**

Hurst

Wedding Witnesses:

David Fitzgerald & William Fraser

- William Humfrey Rankin & Unknown
  - Hamilton Rankin & Harriet Jane Davy – 5 Feb 1874 (Marriage, **St. Peter Parish**)

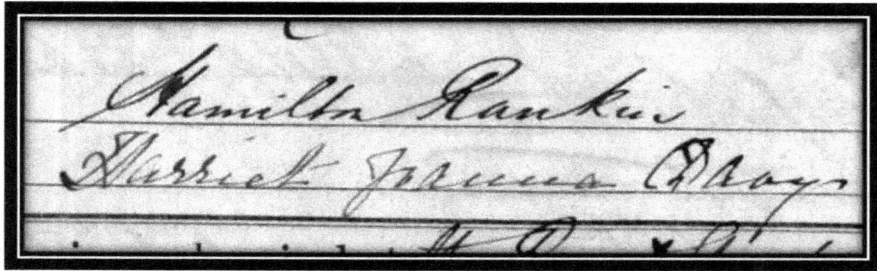

Signatures:

Hamilton Rankin (son):

    Residence - Chisholm House, London - February 5, 1874

    Occupation - Esquire - February 5, 1874

Harriet Jane Davy, daughter of William Davy (daughter-in-law):

    Residence - 13 Heytesbury Street, Kill Galway - February 5, 1874

William Davy (father):

    Occupation - Inland Revenue

William Humfrey Rankin (father):

    Occupation - C. E. [Church of England]

Rankin Surname Ireland: 1600s to 1900s

Wedding Witnesses:

Charles Lloyd & William Davy

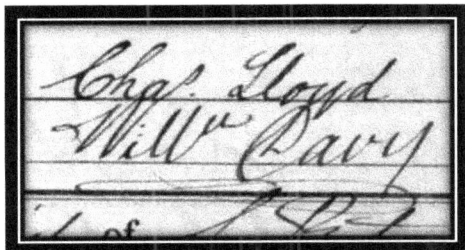

Signatures:

Individual Baptisms/Births

None Were Listed

Individual Burials

- Alexander Rankin – bur. 6 May 1698 (Burial, **St. Audoen Parish**)

- Alexander Rankin – bur. 11 Oct 1727 (Burial, **St. Catherine Parish**)

Alexander Rankin (deceased):

   Age at Death - child

- Bridget Rankin – bur. 15 Nov 1803 (Burial, **Glasnevin Parish**)

Bridget Rankin (deceased):

   Residence - King Street - before November 15, 1803

- Catherine Anne Rankin – b. 1792, d. 28 Oct 1854, bur. 1854 (Burial, **Crumlin Parish**)

Catherine Anne Rankin (deceased):

   Residence - Hilton Lodge, Blackrock - October 28, 1854

   Age at Death - 62 years

- Charles Rankin – b. 1803, d. 23 Dec 1833, bur. 1833 (Burial, **Crumlin Parish**)

Charles Rankin (deceased):

   Residence - Dublin - December 23, 1833

   Age at Death - 30 years

- Deborah Rankin – bur. 14 Oct 1822 (Burial, **Carlow Parish**)

- Elizabeth Rankin – bur. 29 Mar 1773 (Burial, **St. Paul Parish**)

- Elizabeth Rankin – bur. 25 Dec 1803 (Burial, **St. Catherine Parish**)

Elizabeth Rankin (deceased):

Residence - Harold's Cross - before December 25, 1803

- George Rankin – b. 1757, d. 29 Sep 1832, bur. 1832 (Burial, **Crumlin Parish**)

George Rankin (deceased):

Residence - D'Olier Street - September 29, 1832

Age at Death - 75 years

- George Rankin – b. 1784, d. 30 Sep 1854, bur. 1854 (Burial, **Crumlin Parish**)

George Rankin (deceased):

Residence - Richmond Avenue - September 30, 1854

Age at Death - 70 years

- Isabel Rankin – bur. 6 Dec 1818 (Burial, **St. Mary Parish**)

Isabel Rankin (deceased):

Residence - Capel Street - before December 6, 1818

- James Rankin – bur. 26 Mar 1726 (Burial, **St. Catherine Parish**)

James Rankin (deceased):

Age at Death - child

Rankin Surname Ireland: 1600s to 1900s

- James Rankin – bur. 12 Feb 1801 (Burial, **St. Paul Parish**)

- James Rankin – b. Aug 1835, bur. 17 Nov 1836 (Burial, **St. Mark Parish**)

James Rankin (deceased):

   Residence - George's Quay - before November 17, 1836

   Age at Death - 16 months

- Jane Rankin – bur. 21 Apr 1756 (Burial, **St. Catherine Parish**)

- John Rankin – bur. 4 Oct 1806 (Burial, **St. James Parish**)

John Rankin (deceased):

   Residence - Hawkins Street - before October 4, 1806

- John Rankin – d. 4 Nov 1811, bur. 1811 (Burial, **Carlow Parish**)

John Rankin (deceased):

   Occupation - Sexton - November 4, 1811

- John Rankin – b. 1812, bur. 12 Feb 1891 (Burial, **St. George Parish**)

John Rankin (deceased):

   Residence - 5 Sarsfield Street - before February 12, 1891

   Age at Death - 79 years

   Remarks about Death - headstone erected on August 4, 1891

Hurst

- Joseph Rankin – b. 1736, bur. 14 May 1820 (Burial, **St. Catherine Parish**)

Joseph Rankin (deceased):

    Residence - Earl Street - before May 14, 1820

    Age at Death - 84 years

- Lelias Rankin – b. 1815, bur. 14 Nov 1839 (Burial, **St. Peter Parish**)

Lelias Rankin (deceased):

    Residence - Cullen's Wood - before November 14, 1839

    Age at Death - 24 years

    Place of Burial - St. Kevin's Cemetery

- Mary Rankin – bur. 16 Mar 1780 (Burial, **St. Paul Parish**)
- Mary Rankin – bur. 4 Jul 1813 (Burial, **St. Catherine Parish**)

Mary Rankin (deceased):

    Residence - Mulinahack - before July 4, 1813

- Mary Anne Rankin – bur. 31 Oct 1814 (Burial, **St. Paul Parish**)
- Mary Louisa Rankin – b. 1820, d. 9 Jun 1846, bur. 1846 (Burial, **Crumlin Parish**)

Mary Louisa Rankin (deceased):

    Residence - Milltown - June 9, 1846

    Age at Death - 26 years

Rankin Surname Ireland: 1600s to 1900s

- Richard Rankin – bur. 12 Jan 1741 (Burial, **St. Mary Parish**)

- Richard Rankin – b. 1827, bur. 23 Sep 1893 (Burial, **St. George Parish**)

Richard Rankin (deceased):

    Residence - 5 Sarsfield Street - before September 23, 1893

    Age at Death - 66 years

- Robert Rankin – bur. 12 Aug 1810 (Burial, **St. Paul Parish**)

- Samuel Rankin – bur. 29 Jul 1754 (Burial, **St. Catherine Parish**)

- Thomas Rankin – bur. 4 Nov 1802 (Burial, **St. Paul Parish**)

- Thomas Rankin – bur. 19 Oct 1820 (Burial, **St. Mary Parish**)

Thomas Rankin (deceased):

    Residence - Lower Mary Street - before October 19, 1820

- Unknown Rankin – bur. 3 Apr 1772 (Burial, **St. Mark Parish**)

Unknown Rankin (deceased):

    Residence - White's Quay - before April 3, 1772

    Occupation - Captain - before April 3, 1772

- Unknown Rankin (Mr.) – bur. 25 Jul 1742 (Burial, **St. Mary Parish**)

- William Rankin – bur. 23 Jan 1764 (Burial, **St. John Parish**)

- William Rankin – bur. 14 Jan 1771 (Burial, **St. James Parish**)

William Rankin (deceased):

    Residence - Francis Street - before January 14, 1771

Hurst

- William Rankin – bur. 4 Feb 1791 (Burial, **St. Paul Parish**)

- William Rankin – d. 20 Aug 1833, bur. 1833 (Burial, **Crumlin Parish**)

William Rankin (deceased):

Residence - Dublin - August 20, 1833

Individual Marriages

- Beatrice Rankin & Loftus Lounds

    o Amy Lounds – b. 20 Sep 1904, bapt. 11 Oct 1904 (Baptism, **Rathmines Parish (RC)**)

Loftus Lounds (father):

Residence - 89 Grossend Square - October 11, 1904

- Catherine Rankin & Joseph Mitchell – 24 Apr 1856 (Marriage, **St. Mary, Pro Cathedral Parish (RC)**)

    o Catherine Mitchell – b. 22 Oct 1858, bapt. 3 Nov 1858 (Baptism, **St. Mary, Pro Cathedral Parish (RC)**)

    o Mary Anne Mitchell, b. 5 Jul 1860, bapt. 16 Jul 1860 (Baptism, **St. Mary, Pro Cathedral Parish (RC)**) & David McGrath – 18 Jul 1880 (Marriage, **St. Mary, Pro Cathedral Parish (RC)**)

Mary Anne Mitchell (daughter):

Residence - 17 Little Strand Street - July 18, 1880

David McGrath, son of Christopher McGrath & Catherine Kelly (son-in-law):

Residence - 17 Upper Exchange Street - July 18, 1880

Wedding Witnesses:

Peter Golden & Catherine Mitchell

    o Elizabeth Mitchell – b. 31 Jan 1863, bapt. 16 Feb 1863 (Baptism, **St. Mary, Pro Cathedral Parish (RC)**)

Hurst

Joseph Mitchell (father):

Residence - 17 Little Strand Street - November 3, 1858

July 16, 1860

February 16, 1863

Wedding Witnesses:

Andrew Regan & Mary Anne Lee

- Catherine Rankin & Thomas Smith – 20 Jun 1858 (Marriage, **St. Mary Parish (RC)**)

Wedding Witnesses:

John Kelly & Mary Fox

- Christine Rankin & Stephen Hayes
    - Michael Hayes – b. 17 Aug 1882, bapt. 25 Aug 1882 (Baptism, **St. Mary, Pro Cathedral Parish (RC)**)
    - Christine Hayes – b. 27 Feb 1892, bapt. 2 Mar 1892 (Baptism, **St. Mary, Pro Cathedral Parish (RC)**)

Stephen Hayes (father):

Residence - 9 Artisan's Dwellings, Buckingham Street - August 25, 1885

22 Rutland Street Cottages - March 2, 1892

- Elizabeth Rankin & Edward Kernan (K e r n a n)
    - Frederick Joseph Kernan (K e r n a n) – b. 2 Mar 1896, bapt. 6 Mar 1896 (Baptism, **St. Mary, Pro Cathedral Parish (RC)**)

Rankin Surname Ireland: 1600s to 1900s

Edward Kernan (father):

Residence - 61 Lower Gardiner Street - March 6, 1896

- Ellen Rankin & Richard Folkes
  - William Folkes – b. 16 Dec 1857, bapt. 3 Jan 1858 (Baptism, **St. James Parish (RC)**)

Richard Folkes (father):

Residence - 16 Irwin Street - January 3, 1858

- Frances Rankin & Thomas McEnroe
  - Frances McEnroe & John Donohoe – 3 Aug 1862 (Marriage, **St. Catherine Parish (RC)**)

Frances McEnroe (daughter):

Residence - 23 Meath Street - August 3, 1862

John Donohoe, son of Garrett Donohoe & Bridget Kenna (son-in-law):

Residence - 50 Meath Street - August 3, 1862

Wedding Witnesses:

Peter Woods & Mary Anne Woods

- Honor Rankin & Gulielmo Riordan – 10 Jan 1874 (Marriage, **Cork - SS. Peter & Paul Parish (RC)**)

Honor Rankin (wife):

Residence - 4 Peter's Church Lane - January 10, 1874

Gulielmo Riordan (husband):

Residence - 4 Peter's Church Lane - January 10, 1874

Hurst

Wedding Witnesses:

Jane Higgins & Helen Higgins

- Jane Rankin & Alfred Jones

  - George Richard Jones – b. 1877, bapt. 1899 (Baptism, **St. Andrew Parish (RC)**)

Alfred Jones (father):

Residence - 12 Hope Street - 1899

- Jessie Rankin & James Ryan

  - Eleanor Jessie Ryan – b. 21 Sep 1858, bapt. 4 Oct 1858 (Baptism, **St. Agatha Parish (RC)**)

  - Gulielmo Ryan – b. 9 Nov 1860, bapt. 26 Nov 1860 (Baptism, **St. Agatha Parish (RC)**)

  - Michael Ryan – b. 27 Jan 1863, bapt. 4 Feb 1863 (Baptism, **St. Mary, Pro Cathedral Parish (RC)**)

  - David Patrick Ryan – b. 15 Mar 1865, bapt. 12 Apr 1865 (Baptism, **St. Agatha Parish (RC)**)

  - Honor Ryan – b. 2 Jan 1876, bapt. 4 Feb 1876 (Baptism, **St. Mary, Pro Cathedral Parish (RC)**)

  - William Ryan & Julie Scally – 15 May 1904 (Marriage, **St. Mary, Pro Cathedral Parish (RC)**)

William Ryan (son):

Residence - 7 Lower Dominick Street - May 15, 1904

Julie Scally, daughter of Joseph Scally & Margaret Hanlon (daughter-in-law):

Residence - 7 Lower Dominick Street - May 15, 1904

Wedding Witnesses:

Joseph McGerry & Catherine Hand

Rankin Surname Ireland: 1600s to 1900s

James Ryan (father):

Residence - 8 North William Street - October 4, 1858

November 26, 1860

13 Upper Dorset Street - February 4, 1863

14 Portland Row - April 12, 1865

25 Hardwicke Street - February 4, 1876

- Joan Rankin & Thomas Rafferty
    - Nicholas Rafferty – b. 15 Feb 1899, bapt. 17 Feb 1899 (Baptism, **Harrington Street Parish** (RC))

Thomas Rafferty (father):

Residence - 42 Charlemont Street - February 17, 1899

- Margaret Rankin & Charles Brady
    - John Brady – bapt. 28 Jul 1771 (Baptism, **St. Catherine Parish** (RC))
    - Mary Brady – bapt. 1773 (Baptism, **SS. Michael & John Parish** (RC))
    - Jane Brady – bapt. 1774 (Baptism, **SS. Michael & John Parish** (RC))
- Margaret Rankin & Donald Cameron
    - Donald Cameron & Julie Neligan – 29 Jul 1870 (Marriage, **Spa Parish** (RC))

Julie Neligan, daughter of Michael Neligan & Catherine Jones (daughter-in-law):

Residence - Castleisland - July 29, 1870

Wedding Witnesses:

Patrick Higgins & Mary Anne Flaherty

Hurst

- Margaret Rankin & Henry Hunt

  - Margaret Hunt & John Bolton – 14 Aug 1904 (Marriage, **St. Mary, Pro Cathedral Parish** (RC))

Margaret Hunt (daughter):

Residence - 18 Capel Street - August 14, 1904

John Bolton, son of Richard Bolton & Charlotte MacKay (son-in-law):

Residence - 69 Middle King Street - August 14, 1904

Wedding Witnesses:

Bartholomew Jordan & Kathleen Jordan

- Margaret Rankin & John D'Arcy

  - John Joseph D'Arcy – b. 1868, bapt. 1868 (Baptism, **St. Andrew Parish** (RC))

  - Mary Teresa D'Arcy – b. 1869, bapt. 1869 (Baptism, **St. Andrew Parish** (RC))

  - Bridget D'Arcy – b. 1872, bapt. 1872 (Baptism, **St. Andrew Parish** (RC))

John D'Arcy (father):

Residence - 9 Fitzwilliam Place - 1868

1869

1872

- Margaret Rankin & Thomas Kenna

  - Mary Kenna – bapt. 9 Sep 1829 (Baptism, **St. Catherine Parish** (RC))

- Martha Rankin & Patrick Purcell – 2 Aug 1817 (Marriage, **St. Catherine Parish** (RC))

  - Christopher Purcell – bapt. 6 Aug 1818 (Baptism, **St. Catherine Parish** (RC))

Rankin Surname Ireland: 1600s to 1900s

Wedding Witnesses:

Jeremiah Tracy & Anne Purcell

- Mary Rankin & John Burnyeates (B u r n y e a t e s) – 6 Apr 1752 (Marriage, **St. Mark Parish**)

- Mary Anne Rankin & Patrick Lambert

  o Mary Catherine Lambert – b. 19 Feb 1883, bapt. 23 Feb 1883 (Baptism, **St. Mary, Pro Cathedral Parish (RC)**)

  o Francis Lambert – b. 25 Aug 1885, bapt. 31 Aug 1885 (Baptism, **St. Mary, Pro Cathedral Parish (RC)**)

  o Elizabeth Lambert – b. 1888, bapt. 1888 (Baptism, **St. Andrew Parish (RC)**)

  o Joseph Lambert – b. 16 Feb 1889, bapt. 20 Feb 1889 (Baptism, **St. Mary, Pro Cathedral Parish (RC)**)

  o Patrick Joseph Lambert – b. 9 Apr 1891, bapt. 17 Apr 1891 (Baptism, **St. Mary, Pro Cathedral Parish (RC)**)

  o Anne Lambert – b. 19 Nov 1895, bapt. 25 Nov 1895 (Baptism, **St. Mary, Pro Cathedral Parish (RC)**)

Patrick Lambert (father):

Residence - 67 Montgomery Street - February 23, 1883

August 31, 1885

70 Montgomery Street - February 20, 1889

1 Peterson's Lane - 1888

19 Mabbot Street - April 17, 1891

34 Upper Tyrone Street - November 25, 1895

Hurst

- Sarah Rankin & Edward McCann – 22 May 1841 (Marriage, **St. Andrew Parish (RC)**)

Wedding Witnesses:

Matthew McQuirk & Sarah McCann

- Sarah Rankin & James Malone

    o James Joseph Malone – b. 28 Apr 1869, bapt. 6 May 1869 (Baptism, **St. Mary, Pro Cathedral Parish (RC)**)

    o George Malone – b. 21 Oct 1870, bapt. 31 Oct 1870 (Baptism, **St. Mary, Pro Cathedral Parish (RC)**)

    o Mary Teresa Malone – b. 3 Apr 1872, bapt. 5 Apr 1872 (Baptism, **St. Mary, Pro Cathedral Parish (RC)**)

    o Mary Elizabeth Malone – b. 12 Nov 1873, bapt. 24 Nov 1873 (Baptism, **St. Mary, Pro Cathedral Parish (RC)**)

    o Margaret Malone – b. 25 Feb 1875, bapt. 1 Mar 1875 (Baptism, **St. Mary, Pro Cathedral Parish (RC)**)

    o Sarah Jane Malone – b. 10 Feb 1878, bapt. 11 Feb 1878 (Baptism, **St. Mary, Pro Cathedral Parish (RC)**)

    o Bernard (B e r n a r d) James Malone – b. 22 Nov 1879, bapt. 28 Nov 1879 (Baptism, **St. Mary, Pro Cathedral Parish (RC)**)

    o Mary Christine Malone – b. 23 May 1883, bapt. 30 May 1883 (Baptism, **St. Mary, Pro Cathedral Parish (RC)**)

James Malone (father):

Residence - 8 Upper Abbey Street - May 6, 1869

3 Abbey Street - October 31, 1870

53 Stafford Street - April 5, 1872

5 Jervis Street - November 24, 1873

61 Lower Jervis Street - March 1, 1875

November 28, 1879

May 30, 1883

61 Jervis Street - February 11, 1878

Name Variations

Includes Latin and Abbreviated forms of names found in the original documents.

Abigail = Abigale, Abigall

Anne = Ann, Anna, Annae

Bartholomew = Barth, Bartholmeus, Bartholomeo

Bridget = Birgis, Brigid, Brigida, Bridgit

Catherine = Catharine, Catharina, Catharinae, Catherina, Cath, Catha, Cathae, Cathe, Cathn, Kate

Charles = Carolus, Charls, Chas

Christopher = Christoph

Daniel = Danielem, Danielis

Edmund = Edmond

Edward = Ed, Edwd

Eleanor = Eleo, Eleonora, Elinor, Ellenor

Elizabeth = Betty, Elisa, Elisabeth, Eliz, Eliza, Elizab, Elizh, Elizth

Ellen = Elena, Ellena

Emily = Emilia

Esther = Essie, Ester

Francis = Fransicum

George = Geo, Georg, Georgius

Grace = Gratiae

Gulielmo = Guil, Guillelmi, Gulielmum, Guillelmus, Gulmi

Helen = Helena

Rankin Surname Ireland: 1600s to 1900s

Honor = Hanora, Honora

James = Jacobi, Jacobus, Jas

Jane = Joanna

Jeanne = Jeannae, Joannae

Joan = Johanna, Joney

John = Jno, Joannem, Joannes, Johannis

Joseph = Jos

Juliana = Julian

Leticia = Letitia, Lettice, Letticia

Lewis = Louis

Luke = Lucas

Margaret = Margarita, Margaritae, Margeret, Marget, Margt

Martha = Marthae

Mary = Maria, My

Mary Anne = Marianna, Marianne, Maryanne

Michael = Michaelis, Michl

Patrick = Pat, Patt, Patk, Patricii, Patricius

Peter = Petri

Richard = Ricardi, Ricardus, Rich, Richd

Robert = Roberti

Rose = Rosa, Rosae

Thomas = Thom, Thomae, Thoms, Thos, Ths

Timothy = Timotheus, Timy

William = Wil, Will, Willm, Wm

Notes

Notes

Notes

Notes

Notes

Notes

Index

Bolton
John 64
Richard 64
Bradford
Elizabeth 35
Brady
Baptisms
Jane
1774 63
John
1771 Jul 28 63
Mary
1773 63
Charles.. 63
Branagan
Mary 41
Brannick
Catherine...................................... 25
Browne
Margaret 24
Michael Dowd 24
Michael Patrick............................ 8
Burges
Baptisms
Catherine
1878 May 21 13
John Joseph
1876 Apr 16........................ 13
Sarah
1874 Feb 15 13
Births
Catherine
1878 May 12 13

John Joseph
1876 Apr 14........................ 13
Sarah
1874 Feb 9 13
Christopher 13
John 13
Spouses
Sarah 13
Burnyeates
John 65
Byrne
Baptisms
Mary Josephine
1857 Dec 18 32
Births
Mary Josephine
1857 Dec 8 32
Joseph 32
Luke 29
Peter... 32
Thomas 28

Cameron
Donald 63
Families
Donald... 63
Marriages
Donald
1870 Jul 29.......................... 63
Witnesses
Flaherty, Mary Anne 63
Higgins, Patrick............................ 63
Carroll
Roseanne....................................... 21

Clark
  Helen 30
Clarke
  Bridget 20
  Eleanor 32
  Patrick 21
Cleary
  Susan 16
Collins
  Ellen 27
Connor
  Anne 15
Corcoran
  Michael 12
Cunningham
  Andrew 20
  Helena Parker Catto 19
Curran
  Jane 27

D'Arcy
  Baptisms
    Bridget
      1872 64
    John Joseph
      1868 64
    Mary Teresa
      1869 64
  Births
    Bridget
      1872 64
    John Joseph
      1868 54
    Mary Teresa
      1869 64
    John 64
Daly
  Roseanne 38
Davy
  Harriet Jane 50

  William 50
Deegan
  Sarah 13
Denham
  Victoria 15
Donohoe
  Garrett 61
  John 61
Dunn
  Mary 13

Ennis
  Christopher 15
  John 15
  Julianne 14
  Mary Jane 15

Field
  Bartholomew 33
  Roseanne 33
Flanagan
  Elizabeth 38
  Nicholas 38
Folkes
  Baptisms
    William
      1858 Jan 3 61
  Births
    William
      1857 Dec 16 61
    Richard 61

Gray
Anne 37

H

Hanlon
Margaret 62
Hayes
  Baptisms
    Christine
      1892 Mar 2 60
    Michael
      1882 Aug 25 60
  Births
    Christine
      1892 Feb 27 60
    Michael
      1882 Aug 17 60
    Stephen 60
Hearn
Arabella 10
Hughes
  Baptisms
    Edward Christopher
      1866 Jun 4 14
    George Lawrence
      1867 Nov 18 15
    James
      1869 May 31 15
    John
      1877 Jul 23 15
    John Dominick
      1875 Jun 21 15
    Sarah
      1873 Feb 24 15
  Births
    Edward Christopher
      1866 May 28 14

    George Lawrence
      1867 Nov 13 15
    James
      1869 May 21 15
    John
      1877 Jul 13 15
    John Dominick
      1875 Jun 15 15
    Sarah
      1873 Feb 16 15
  Edward 16
  Families
    Edward Christopher 14
    Joseph G. 15
  James 41
  John 14
  Marriages
    Edward Christopher
      1888 Feb 8 14
    Joseph G.
      1901 Jan 20 15
    Witnesses
      Cullen, Thomas 15
      Ennis, John 15
      McKenna, Margaret 15
      Walsh, Catherine 15
  Spouses
    Elizabeth 16
  Thomas Edmond 40
Hunt
Henry 64
Marriages
  Margaret
    1904 Aug 14 64
  Witnesses
    Jordan, Bartholomew 64
    Jordan, Kathleen 64

J

Jenkinson
John 46

Thomas Rawson 45
Jessop
Anne 11
Jones
Alfred 62
Baptisms
George Richard
1899 62
Births
George Richard
1877 62
Catherine 63

K

Kathrens
Charlotte 1
Kelly
Catherine 59
Kenna
Baptisms
Mary
1829 Sep 9 64
Bridget 61
Thomas 64
Kernan
Baptisms
Frederick Joseph
1896 Mar 6 60
Births
Frederick Joseph
1896 Mar 2 60
Edward 60
King
Bridget 29

L

Lambert
Baptisms

Anne
1895 Nov 25 65
Elizabeth
1888 65
Francis
1885 Aug 31 65
Joseph
1889 Feb 20 65
Mary Catherine
1883 Feb 23 65
Patrick Joseph
1891 Apr 17 65
Births
Anne
1895 Nov 19 65
Elizabeth
1888 65
Francis
1885 Aug 25 65
Joseph
1889 Feb 16 65
Mary Catherine
1883 Feb 19 65
Patrick Joseph
1891 Apr 9 65
Patrick 65
Lounds
Baptisms
Amy
1904 Oct 11 59
Births
Amy
1904 Sep 20 59
Loftus 59
Lynch
Harriet 47
Michael 47

M

Mac Mullen
George Read 21

Robert 21

MacKay
Charlotte 64

Magee
Arthur 25
John 26

Magrath
Mary 38

Malone
Baptisms
George
1870 Oct 31 66
James Joseph
1869 May 6 66
Margaret
1875 Mar 1 66
Mary Christine
1883 May 30 66
Mary Elizabeth
1873 Nov 24 66
Mary Teresa
1872 Apr 5 66
Sarah Jane
1878 Feb 11 66
Births
Bernard (B e r n a r d) James
1879 Nov 22 66
1879 Nov 28 66
George
1870 Oct 21 66
James Joseph
1869 Apr 28 66
Margaret
1875 Feb 25 66
Mary Christine
1883 May 23 66
Mary Elizabeth
1873 Nov 12 66
Mary Teresa
1872 Apr 3 66
Sarah Jane
1878 Feb 10 66
James 66

Martin

Anne 17, 38
Bartholomew 9
Henry 17
Mary 23
Richard 9

Mauchan
Margaret 26

Maunsell
Mary Louisa 49

McCann
Edward 66

McCormick
Rose 33

McEnroe
Marriages
Frances
1862 Aug 3 61
Witnesses
Woods, Mary Anne 61
Woods, Peter 61
Thomas 61

McGrath
Christopher 59
David 59

Minion
Nathaniel 36
Rebecca S. 36

Mitchell
Baptisms
Catherine
1858 Nov 3 59
Elizabeth
1863 Feb 16 59
Mary Anne
1860 Jul 16 59
Births
Catherine
1858 Oct 22 59
Elizabeth
1863 Jan 31 59
Mary Anne
1860 Jul 5 59
Joseph 59
Marriages

Mary Anne
   1880 Jul 18 59
Witnesses
   Catherine.. 59
   Golden, Peter 59
Monahan
  Ellen 24
Mooney
  Isabel 12

N

Neligan
  Julie 63
  Michael.. 63
Nicholson
  Elizabeth.. 35

P

Parr
  Catherine Anne.. 21
Purcell
  Baptisms
   Christopher
    1818 Aug 6 64
   Patrick.. 64

R

Rafferty
  Baptisms
   Nicholas
    1899 Feb 17 63
  Births
   Nicholas
    1899 Feb 15 63
   Thomas 63

Rankin
  Baptisms
   Abigail
    1810 Mar 11.................................... 41
   Alexander
    1834 Dec 10 1
   Allen Ponsonby
    1879 Jun 10...................................... 2
   Andrew
    1893 Sep 10 22
   Anne
    1859 Dec 16 23
    1869 17
   Anne Georgina
    1870 May 8 11
   Bridget
    1866 Sep 24 24
    1872 Feb 9 17
   Catherine
    1874 Sep 9 41
   Catherine Anne
    1879 Jul 30.................................... 26
   Catherine Macgregor
    1874 Oct 9 2
   Charlotte Anne
    1861 Apr 24 12
   Christian
    1751 Apr 1 27
    1761 Jan 25.................................... 11
   David William
    1866 Aug 12 5
   Elizabeth
    1766 Dec 15 40
    1789 40
    1835 33
    1838 32
    1869 Feb 17 24
    1877 Jan 29.................................... 25
    1878 Oct 9..................................... 33
    1889 Mar 27..................................... 6
   Elizabeth Constance
    1860 Sep 30................................... 37
   Elizabeth Jane
    1868 May 30 5

Elizabeth Louisa
1874 Jan 14 5
Elizabeth Maude
1896 Oct 9 22
Ellen
1820 Jul 2 44
Emily Beatrice
1877 Sep 5 5
Esther
1756 May 27 27
Eva Isabel
1885 Apr 2 42
Frances Rebecca
1883 Mar 16 45
Francis
1864 17
1864 Mar 30 23
1895 Sep 9 16
George
1870 Aug 1 24
George Joseph
1899 Feb 13 38
George Samuel
1863 Nov 11 12
Harold Douglas
1884 Mar 28 2
Harriet
1881 Oct 26 26
Henry
1872 Feb 7 5
James
1738 Apr 9 1
1759 Mar 1 27
1765 May 12 40
1844 Mar 5 28
1862 Aug 24 30
1894 Dec 5 25
Jane
1755 May 20 27
1807 Dec 7 41
Jane Emily
1845 Mar 12 10
Jessie Violet
1862 Jun 25 4

John
1760 Jun 21 27
1834 Jul 11 13
1870 Nov 20 32
1876 Apr 19 24
1879 Jan 27 33
1889 Oct 6 31
John David
1900 Dec 9 44
Joseph Patrick
1873 Jul 9 26
Margaret
1738 Dec 17 26
1806 Jan 19 12
1835 Jun 30 13
1840 Dec 27 44
Mary
1740 Oct 10 45
1823 Aug 10 44
1824 Mar 28 11
1830 32
1861 Nov 25 23
1895 Jul 14 4
Mary A.
1838 Aug 20 13
Mary Emily
1860 17
Mary Jane
1875 Sep 18 20
Mary Rebecca
1887 May 18 45
Michael
1879 Feb 17 24
Nora Amelia Minnie
1876 Nov 2 2
Patrick
1872 41
1874 Mar 16 24
Patrick R.
1866 17
Richard
1872 Aug 27 24
Richard Joseph
1880 Aug 23 22

Richard Patrick
  1897 Oct 22 38
Sarah Jane
  1889 Mar 27 6
Spencer Wilson
  1881 Jul 22 2
Susan
  1757 Nov 6 27
Teresa
  1809 Oct 22 44
Thomas
  1834 May 21 26
Vincent James
  1899 Jul 31 35
Violet May
  1900 Dec 23 49
Walter George
  1891 Jun 30 19
William
  1761 Sep 13 27
  1817 May 19 31
  1834 Jan 31 27
  1859 Jan 9 37
William Henry
  1866 Nov 2 12
  1870 Jan 29 5

Births
Abigail
  1810 41
Allen Ponsonby
  1879 Apr 23 2
Andrew
  1893 Jul 27 22
Anne
  1859 Dec 4 23
  1868 17
Anne Georgina
  1870 Apr 26 11
Bridget
  1866 Sep 21 24
  1872 Feb 6 17
Catherine
  1874 Sep 6 41
Catherine Anne

  1792 53
  1879 Jul 25 26
Catherine Macgregor
  1874 Sep 9 2
Charles
  1803 53
Charlotte Anne
  1861 Jan 24 12
David William
  1866 Jun 6 5
Elizabeth
  1789 40
  1869 Feb 15 24
  1877 Jan 24 25
  1878 Oct 7 33
  1886 Jun 28 6
Elizabeth Constance
  1860 Sep 2 37
Elizabeth Jane
  1868 May 9 5
Elizabeth Louisa
  1873 Nov 25 5
Elizabeth Maude
  1896 Sep 13 22
Emily Beatrice
  1877 Jun 15 5
Frances Rebecca
  1883 Mar 2 45
Francis
  1863 17
  1864 Feb 24 23
  1895 Sep 3 16
George
  1757 54
  1784 54
  1870 Jul 29 24
George Joseph
  1899 Feb 6 38
George Samuel
  1863 Sep 20 12
Harold Douglas
  1884 Feb 5 2
Harriet
  1881 Oct 22 26

Hurst

Henry
  1871 Nov 1 5
James
  1835 Aug 55
  1843 Jul 6 28
  1849 May 12 30
  1894 Nov 4 25
Jane
  1807 41
Jane Emily
  1845 Mar 4 10
Jessie Violet
  1862 Jun 4 4
John 32
  1812 55
  1852 Nov 16 32
  1876 Apr 11 24
  1879 Jan 22 33
  1889 Sep 27 31
John David
  1900 Dec 8 44
Joseph
  1736 56
Joseph Patrick
  1873 Jul 5 26
Lelias
  1815 56
Margaret
  1840 Dec 27 44
Mary
  1823 Aug 3 44
  1861 Nov 16 23
  1895 Jul 8 4
Mary Emily
  1860 17
Mary Jane
  1875 Sep 15 20
Mary Louisa
  1820 56
Mary Rebecca
  1887 May 14 45
Michael
  1879 Feb 11 24
Nora Amelia Minnie

  1876 Sep 30 2
Patrick
  1872 41
  1874 Mar 12 24
Patrick R.
  1866 17
Richard
  1827 57
  1872 Aug 27 24
Richard Joseph
  1880 Aug 16 22
Richard Patrick
  1897 Oct 20 38
Sarah Jane
  1889 Oct 11 6
Spencer Wilson
  1881 Jun 15 2
Teresa
  1809 Oct 13 44
Thomas
  1837 Sep 1837 39
Vincent James
  1899 Jul 19 35
Violet May
  1900 Nov 15 49
Walter George
  1891 May 26 19
William Henry
  1865 Aug 22 12
  1869 Nov 14 5

Burials
Alexander
  1698 May 6 53
  1727 Oct 11 53
Bridget
  1803 Nov 15 53
Catherine Anne
  1854 53
Charles
  1833 53
Deborah
  1822 Oct 14 53
Elizabeth
  1773 Mar 29 54

1803 Dec 25	54
George	
1832	54
1854	54
Henry	
1873 Sep 10	5
Isabel	
1818 Dec 6	54
James	
1726 Mar 26	54
1801 Feb 12	55
1836 Nov 17	55
Jane	
1756 Apr 21	55
John	
1806 Oct 4	55
1811	55
1891 Feb 12	55
Joseph	
1826 May 14	56
Lelias	
1839 Nov 14	56
Mary	
1780 Mar 16	56
1813 Jul 4	56
Mary Anne	
1814 Oct 31	56
Mary Louisa	
1846	56
Richard	
1741 Jan 12	57
1893 Sep 23	57
Robert	
1810 Aug 12	57
Samuel	
1754 Jul 29	57
Thomas	
1802 Nov 4	57
1820 Oct 19	57
Unknown	
1772 Apr 3	57
Unknown (Mr.)	
1742 Jul 25	57
William	

1764 Jan 23	57
1771 Jan 14	57
1791 Feb 4	58
1833	58
Deaths	
Catherine Anne	
1854 Oct 28	53
Charles	
1833 Dec 23	53
George	
1832 Sep 29	54
1854 Sep 30	54
John	
1811 Nov 4	55
Mary Louisa	
1846 Jun 9	56
Samuel James	
bef. 1895 May 13	40
William	
1833 Aug 20	58
Families	
Alexander	1
Charles	1, 2
Charles Edward	4
David	4, 6, 7
Dionysius	20
Edward	8, 9
Francis	10
George 11, 12, 13, 14, 16, 17, 18, 19	
George Joseph	38
Gulielmo	20
Hamilton	21, 50
Henry	22, 23, 24
Hugh	25
James 25, 26, 27, 28, 36	
John	31, 32, 33
John Turnbull (T u r n b u l l)	30
Joseph	35
Leslie	36
Nathaniel	37
Peter	37
Richard	17, 38
Robert	39, 40

Hurst

Samuel James.. 40

Sydney 33

Thomas 41

Thomas Andrew 47

Unknown..41, 42, 43

William 44, 45, 47

William Henry 19, 49

William Humfrey 50

William Humphrey 49

George 42

James 42

Marriages

Anne

    1879 Oct 19.. 23

Beatrice 59

Catherine

    1856 Apr 24... 59

    1858 Jun 20... 60

Charles

    1826 Jan 22... 1

    1856 Aug 30 2

Charlotte Anne

    1883 Sep 27... 18

Christine.. 60

Dionysius

    1873 Jul 1 20

Elizabeth 60

    1856 Nov 25.. 32

    1878 Apr 12... 7

    1901 Feb 13 25

Elizabeth Jane

    1885 Feb 17... 48

Ellen 61

Emily Anne

    1845 Oct 9... 21

Euphemia

    1855 Feb 20... 28

Frances 61

Francis

    1843 Sep 8... 10

George

    1753 May 22 13

George Joseph

    1893 Jun 25... 38

Georgina

    1895 May 13 40

Hamilton

    1820 Jul 8.. 21

    1874 Feb 5 50

Henry

    1857 Jan 13... 23

    1897 Mar 2 24

Honor

    1874 Jan 10 61

James

    1786 Dec 1 27

    1899 Dec 9 36

Jane 62

Jessie 62

Jessie Violet

    1884 Sep 29 4

Joan 63

John

    1877 Nov 25.. 33

John Turnbull (T u r n b u l l)

    1857 Jan 12 30

Joseph

    1768 Sep 2 35

Julia Anne

    1875 Oct 26 9

Margaret.. 63, 64

    1858 May 9 14

Martha

    1817 Aug 2 64

Mary

    1752 Apr 6.. 65

    1846 Jan 10... 8

    1866 Feb 11 14

    1870 Oct 14... 12

Mary Anne 65

Peter

    1835 Dec 26.. 37

Richard

    1860 Jan 22... 17

    1895 Aug 5 38

Robert

    1840 Dec 14 39

Sarah 66

Rankin Surname Ireland: 1600s to 1900s

1841 May 22	66
1862 Nov 5	35
1866 Aug 26	13
Sydney	
1867 Aug 27	33
Thomas Andrew	
1883 Dec 16	47
Violet Elizabeth	
1869 Apr 5	45
William	
1713 Jul 2	44
1806 Feb 18	44
William Henry	
1891 Feb 1	19
William Humphrey	
1845 Feb 22	49

Witnesses

Armstrong (A r m s t r o n g), David	3
Bannington, Margaret	10
Bayly, Henry	39
Bowen, Arthur	8
Carr, Elizabeth	19
Carr, Richard	19
Connor, John	17
Courtenay, Mary	9
Courtenay, Thomas	9
Crawford, John J.	22
Cullen, Catherine	16
Cullen, Hannah	38
Cunningham, Andrew	20
Curran, Hannah	27
Davy, William	51
Dunne, Bernard (B e r n a r d)	12
Eagan, Francis	12
Edmund	5
Field, Henry	33
Field, Teresa	33
Fitzgerald, David	50
Fox, Edward	34
Fox, Mary	60
Fraser, William	50
George	22
Goff, Michael	44

Gormley (G o r m l e y), Michael	25
Hanlon, Michael	46
Hearn (H e a r n), George	11
Henderson, Charles Robert	5
Henry	23
Higgins, Helen	62
Higgins, Jane	62
Jeffares, Jeannie	37
Jones, Matthew	37
Kavanagh, Michael	14
Kelly, John	60
Kenny, Edward	49
Kinahan, Joseph	24
Kirwan, Elizabeth	48
Lamb, Maurice	27
Lambert, Mary	24
Lee, Mary Anne	60
Lloyd, Charles	51
Lynch, Patrick	48
MacDonald, John	49
Maher, Bridget	26
Malone, John	30
Martin, Anne	25
Mary	23
McCann, Sarah	66
McDermott (M c D e r m o t t), Margaret	17
McQuirk, Matthew	66
Minion, Thomas	37
Moore, John	21
Mulvey, Mary	14
Murphy, Peter	39
Murphy, Thomas	41
Murray, Anne	21
Nugent, Edward	11
O'Brien, Frances	41
O'Brien, Gulielmo	16
O'Connor, Thomas	30, 31
O'Gare, Edward	13
O'Hagan, Mary Anne	13
Purcell, Anne	65
Read, Mary	39
Regan, Andrew	60
Reilly, Margaret	12

Hurst

Reynart, Julie 37
Richard 38
Sharp, Christopher 1
Sinclair, John 31
Spring, John 26
Straeman, Priscilla 36
Strange, Anne 44
Thorpe, Thomas Edward 20
Tracy, Jeremiah 65
Walsh, John E. 39
Walsh,, Michael 10
Webb, Andrew 34
Wheatley, Margery 8
Whelan, Peter 32
White, Margaret 32
William 1, 46
William T. 39
Wilson, Joseph S. 3
Wingate, James 36
R. B. 43
Spouses
Agnes 31
Anne 4
Catherine 26, 41
Elizabeth 6, 11, 22
Harriet Elizabeth 12
Helen 22
Jane 41
Janet 44
Julianne 13
Mary 40
Mary A. 1
Mary Jane 37
Rebecca 45
Sarah 14, 40
Susan 45
Violet May 49
Susan 43
T. George 43
W. H. 43
Reid
George 48
John 48

Renwick
Catherine 26
Reynolds
Alice 44
Richardson
Alexander Lindesay 4
Effingham L. 4
Riordan
Gulielmo 61
Roy
Andrew 35
James 35
Ryan
Baptisms
David Patrick
  1865 Apr 12 62
Eleanor Jessie
  1858 Oct 4 62
Gulielmo
  1860 Nov 26 62
Honor
  1876 Feb 4 62
Michael
  1863 Feb 4 62
Births
David Patrick
  1865 Mar 15 62
Eleanor Jessie
  1858 Sep 21 62
Gulielmo
  1860 Nov 9 62
Honor
  1876 Jan 2 62
Michael
  1863 Jan 27 62
Families
William 62
James 62
Marriages
William
  1904 May 15 62
Witnesses
Hand, Catherine 62
McGerry, Joseph 62

S

Sands
- Joseph 18
- Thomas James 18

Scally
- Joseph 62
- Julie 62

Shaw
- Elizabeth 22

Sheerin
- Julie 23

Sillery
- **Baptisms**
  - George
    - *1886* 23
  - William Francis
    - *1885 Jan 7* 23
- **Births**
  - George
    - *1886* 23
  - William Francis
    - *1885 Jan 5* 23
  - Henry 23
  - William 23

Sinclair
- **Baptisms**
  - Sarah Mary
    - *1895 Sep 7* 28
- **Births**
  - Sarah Mary
    - *1895 Oct 4* 28
  - John 28
- **Marriages**
  - Sarah Mary
    - *1895 Sep 8* 28
  - **Witnesses**
    - Canan, Michael 29
    - Jane 29

Smith
- Thomas 60

Stone
- Elizabeth 20

Strade
- Anne 44

Strait
- Anne 44

U

Unknown 2, 7, 8, 9, 17, 18, 19, 21, 28, 33, 35, 36, 40, 42, 43, 45, 47, 50
- Anne 39
- Catherine 31
- Christian 26, 27
- Elizabeth 25, 32, 33
- Ellen 33
- Hannah 11
- Julie 12
- Margaret 12
- Martha 1
- Mary 4, 28, 44
- Sarah 33, 40

W

Walsh
- Anne Isabel 39

Walshe
- Michael Henry 7
- Patrick 7

Ward
- **Baptisms**
  - Mary Teresa
    - *1859 Apr 8* 14
  - Sarah Catherine
    - *1862 Jan 24* 14
- **Births**
  - Mary Teresa
    - *1859 Mar 22* 14
  - Sarah Catherine
    - *1862 Jan 17* 14

Hurst

Gulielmo 14

Margaret 38

Patrick.. 38

Spouses

    Anne.. 14

Thomas 14

Wheatley

Elizabeth 33

William 34

Wilson

Births

  Jane Ponsonby

    1837 2

Thomas 3

About The Author

Donovan Hurst graduated from San Diego State University with a Bachelor of Arts in the major field of studies of History and a minor in the field of studies of Anthropology. He is a current member of The General Society of Mayflower Descendants and has been conducting genealogical research for over 10 years tracing back his ancestors to their ancestral homelands in Denmark, England, France, Germany, Ireland, Norway, and Scotland.

www.ingramcontent.com/pod-product-compliance
Lightning Source LLC
Chambersburg PA
CBHW081158270326
41930CB00014B/3205